W9-CNL-527

Prentice Hall Guides
to Advanced Communication

Guide to
Presentations

Mary Munter
Tuck School of Business
Dartmouth College

Lynn Russell
Professional Development Company

PRENTICE HALL
Upper Saddle River, New Jersey 07458

Library of Congress Cataloging-in-Publication Data
Munter, Mary.
  Guide to presentations / Mary Munter, Lynn Russell. — 1st ed.
    p. cm.
  ISBN 0-13-035132-6
  1. Business presentations. I. Russell, Lynn. II. Title.
HF5718.22 .M86 2001
658.4'5—dc21

                                    2001021992

Editor-in-Chief: Jeff Shelstad
Assistant Editor: Jennifer Surich
Editorial Assistant: Virginia Sheridan
Media Project Manager: Michele Faranda
Senior Marketing Manager: Debbie Clare
Marketing Assistant: Brian Rappelfeld
Managing Editor (Production): Judy Leale
Production Editor: Theresa Festa
Production Assistant: Keri Jean
Permissions Coordinator: Suzanne Grappi
Associate Director, Manufacturing: Vincent Scelta
Production Manager: Arnold Vila
Design Manager: Patricia Smythe
Designer: Steve Frim
Art Director: Jayne Conte
Cover Design: Kiwi Design
Associate Director, Multimedia Production: Karen Goldsmith
Manager, Print Production: Christy Mahon
Composition: Rainbow Graphics
Full-Service Project Management: Rainbow Graphics
Printer/Binder: Victor Graphics, Inc.

Credits and acknowledgments borrowed from other sources and reproduced, with permission, in this textbook appear on appropriate page within text.

Copyright © 2002 by Pearson Education, Inc., Upper Saddle River, New Jersey, 07458. All rights reserved. Printed in the United States of America. This publication is protected by Copyright and permission should be obtained from the publisher prior to any prohibited reproduction, storage in a retrieval system, or transmission in any form or by any means, electronic, mechanical, photocopying, recording, or likewise. For information regarding permission(s), write to: Rights and Permission Department.

20 19 18 17 16 15 14 13 12 11
ISBN 0-13-035132-6

Table of Contents

PART I
PRESENTATION
STRATEGY

CHAPTER 1

CHAPTER 2

CHAPTER 3

PART II
PRESENTATION
IMPLEMENTATION

Introduction

HOW THIS BOOK CAN HELP YOU

If you have a specific question about presentations, turn to the relevant part of this book for guidance. For example:

- You're anxious about an upcoming presentation. How can you calm yourself down?

- You think you did a decent job on your presentation, but you're not sure if it will get the desired results. How can you come up with a presentation objective that focuses your efforts and enables you to measure your results?

- Your boss seemed to totally miss the point of your last presentation. How can you aim your message so that it reaches your boss? How can you make sure your key points don't get lost?

- You're giving a sales presentation. How can you be certain the audience will understand the benefits of your recommendation? What strategies can you use to get them to say "yes"?

- You're presenting to an unknown audience. What sort of first impression will you make? How can you enhance your credibility?

- Audience members appear to be confused, frustrated, or sleepy as they look to your computer-generated slide show. How can you design slides that broadcast your message, highlight key data, and hold the interest of the group?

- Someone in the audience seems to be attacking you. How can you handle a hostile audience member or hostile questions?
- You do a fine job discussing your ideas when you are sitting down at a meeting, but as soon as you have to stand up in front of a group, you feel awkward. What should you do with your hands and feet in formal situations and in less formal ones?

If you don't have a specific question, but need general guidelines, procedures, and techniques, read through this entire book. For example:

- You want a framework for thinking strategically about presentations.
- You want to know more about the step-by-step process of creating a presentation, from collecting information and asking questions to rehearsing and delivering your talk.
- You want a procedure to use the next time you have to create slides or other visual aids.

If you are taking a professional course, a college course, a workshop, or a seminar, use this book as a reference. You may be a skilled presenter already, but we hope you will find information in this book that will help you polish your skills.

WHO CAN USE THIS BOOK

This book was written for you if you need to make presentations in a business, government, or academic setting—that is, if you need to present yourself and your ideas to achieve results. You may already know these facts:

- *Public speaking is the # 1 fear in the United States.* Many people avoid giving presentations or simply suffer through them. Understanding how to prepare and practice can make presentations far less troubling.
- *Your success is based on communication.* Studies have linked career advancement with the ability to communicate. Your presentation skills are particularly noticeable—by your boss, your co-workers, your clients, and others.
- *Presenting today is more challenging than in the past.* Recent trends such as increased globalization and new presentation technologies make designing and delivering presentations more challenging than ever.

WHY THIS BOOK WAS WRITTEN

The thousands of participants in various professional presentation courses and workshops we have taught—between the two of us, at Columbia, Dartmouth's Tuck, NYU's Stern, and Stanford business schools, as well as at hundreds of companies and organizations—tell us they want a brief summary of presentation techniques. Such busy professionals have found other books on this subject too long or too remedial for their needs. That's why Prentice Hall is publishing this series, the Prentice Hall Guides to Advanced Communication—brief, practical, reader-friendly guides for people who communicate in professional contexts. (See the opening page in this book for more information on the series.)

- *Brief:* The book summarizes key ideas only. Culling from thousands of pages of text and research, we have omitted bulky examples, cases, footnotes, exercises, and discussion questions.

- *Practical:* This book offers clear, straightforward tools you can use. It includes only information you will find useful in a professional context.

- *Reader-friendly:* We have tried to provide an easy-to-skim format—using a direct, matter-of-fact, and nontheoretical tone.

HOW THIS BOOK IS ORGANIZED

The book is divided into two main sections.

Part I: Presentation Strategy (Chapters 1-3)

Effective presentations are based on effective presentation strategy. Effective presentation strategy, in turn, is based on the three strategic variables covered in this first part, which we refer to as the "AIM" strategy for Audience, Intent, and Message.

- *Chapter 1: Analyzing Your Audience.* This chapter covers how to answer the questions: (1) Who are they? (2) What do they know and expect? and (3) What do they feel?

- *Chapter 2: Identifying Your Intent.* In this chapter, you will learn to set your presentation objective, select the appropriate level of audience interaction, and choose the appropriate medium (e.g., presentation, meeting, videoconference, etc.)

- *Chapter 3: Making Your Message Memorable.* To craft a memorable message, refer to the emphasis and persuasion techniques explained in this chapter.

Part II: Presentation Implementation (Chapters 4-6)

Based on your strategy, you can implement an effective presentation, using the three sets of skills described in Part II, which we refer to as the "SVN" implementation framework: Structure, Visuals, and Non-verbal delivery.

- *Chapter 4: Structuring Your Presentation.* This chapter covers what you say during the presentation—organizational techniques to research ideas for your message and verbal techniques to structure your message.

- *Chapter 5: Designing Your Visual Aids.* In this chapter, we take you through the process of creating visual aids by (1) selecting the right equipment, (2) composing message titles, (3) choosing your chart design, (4) ensuring consistency (including templates), and (5) striving for simplicity and readability (including use of color).

- *Chapter 6: Refining Your Nonverbal Delivery.* The final aspect of presentation implementation consists of your nonverbal delivery skills—how you look and sound to your audience. This chapter covers techniques for (1) analyzing the various aspects of your nonverbal delivery, (2) enhancing your delivery, including practice techniques, and (3) relaxing and managing your nervous symptoms.

ACKNOWLEDGMENTS

Thanks to the many people who helped us with this book. *MM:* I am grateful to the thousands of the executives and students I've been privileged to teach; to my colleagues at MCA and ABC; and, most of all, to Paul Argenti. *LR:* Thanks to my husband, colleague, and the best teacher I know, Professor Irv Schenkler of the Stern School of Business at NYU. Thanks also to my extraordinary business partner, teaching partner, and friend, Joann Baney; to the many colleagues who have assisted me at Columbia University, including Tom Ference, Breanna

Kirk, Lisa Kohn, Gerry Lewis, Gwenn Pasco, Ora Shtull, and Martha Stodt; to the MBAs, PhDs, and executives who have taken my courses and workshops; and to my colleagues from other institutions—starting with Mary Munter and including, Paul Argenti, Nancy Keeshan, Chris Kelly, Georgia Kingsley, Bob Reinheimer, Jane Seskin, and Gene Zelazny. You have been great teachers. I have learned much about communication from all of you.

Finally, we would like to acknowledge our sources listed in the bibliography.

Mary Munter
Tuck School of Business
Dartmouth College

Lynn Russell
Professional Development Company

PART I

Strategy Framework

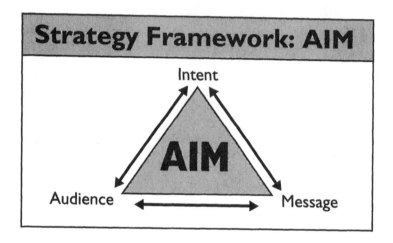

PART I

Presentation Strategy

When people begin an oral presentation, they often think first about how nervous they feel or which template to use on their visuals or what they will wear. Too often, they don't think they can spare the time to consider key aspects of their strategy before they make a presentation. We liken this attitude to saying "Ready . . . Fire!" without taking "Aim."

To avoid misfires in your presentations, attend to each of the three elements of AIM strategy (illustrated on the facing page) before you decide what you want to say.

- **A** stands for "analyzing your audience" (Chapter 1)
- **I** stands for "identifying your intent" (Chapter 2)
- **M** stands for "making your message memorable" (Chapter 3)

What you determine about your strategy—who will be in your audience, how interactive you want to be, how you can be persuasive—will ultimately drive the implementation concerns (structure, visuals, and nonverbal delivery), covered in the second part of this book.

As you can see from the AIM illustration, the three components do not necessarily occur in lockstep order. The arrows show that all three of them interact. For example, your audience affects your choice of persuasive technique and what you intend to accomplish influences how you'll emphasize your message.

CHAPTER I OUTLINE

I. WHO ARE THEY?
   1. Analyzing the primary audience
   2. Analyzing the key influencers
   3. Analyzing the secondary audience

II. WHAT DO THEY KNOW AND EXPECT?
   1. What do they know about the topic?
   2. What do they know about you?
   3. What do they expect in terms of format?
   4. What do they expect in terms of culture?

III. WHAT DO THEY FEEL?
   1. Are they interested?
   2. What is their bias?
   3. Are you asking for a little or a lot?

CHAPTER I

Analyzing Your Audience

One of the three important components of your AIM strategy is to analyze your audience. Good audience analysis requires going beyond your initial assumptions and gathering information about the people who will be listening to and be affected by your presentation. Much of what you need to know can be learned from getting detailed answers to three broad questions covered in this chapter: (1) Who are they? (2) What do they know and expect? (3) What do they feel?

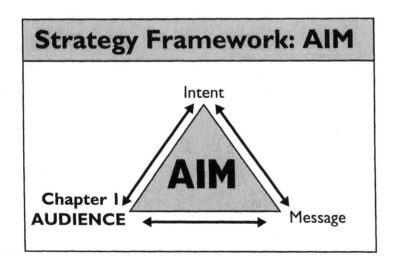

I. WHO ARE THEY?

The first question encourages you to find out as much as you can about your audience—including demographic data about the group and specific information about the individuals. Audience analysis includes both your (1) "primary audience," those who will actually be in the room listening to the presentation, as well as your (2) "secondary (or hidden) audience," those who will hear about it, be affected by it, or be a part of preparing it.

Although most of your work for audience analysis occurs before you prepare your talk, remember to keep collecting information even on the day of the presentation—meet the people who arrive early, watch for reactions to what you say, and listen carefully to the questions people ask.

Analyzing the primary audience

- *As a group:* Asking the "Who are they?" question usually gives you information about the size of the audience, their age range, their educational or work backgrounds, and other demographic information such as gender, race, and culture. With follow-up questions, you may be able to learn much more. For example: What does the group tend to like in terms of delivery style? Do they have different levels of fluency with the language you will be using? Is this a talkative group? An informal one? And so on. The more specific your questions, the more information you'll be able to collect and consider.

- *As individuals:* Use a similar process to collect data and clarify assumptions about individuals. Given your time constraints and relationship with the audience, you should learn as much as possible about specific members of the group. If possible, talk to people who will actually be in the audience; ask them about their experience, their preferences, and their views. As another option, talk to someone who knows the group; this person may be able to help you learn more about various individuals.

Analyzing the key influencers   These individuals control the decision-making process and help shape the group's views.

- *Key decision makers:* Key decision makers are those with direct power or influence. Whenever you can gather specific information about these individuals, you'll have a much easier time targeting your presentation. Try to discover which types of appeals seem to impress them and which types they seem to ignore. Also realize that assessing key decision makers tends to be much easier if you've presented to them before.

- *Opinion leaders:* You will also benefit if you have information about individuals who influence the group indirectly. Try to figure out if they are for or against your ideas. In addition, take some time to assess how the opinion leader manages to influence the group's views.

Analyzing the secondary audience   Secondary audiences are often overlooked. They shouldn't be. These hidden audience members can easily influence your presentation. Therefore, ask yourself: "Who else may hear or see the messages intended for my primary audience?" and "How may these people react to what they hear or see?"

- *Gaining allies:* Often presentations have a ripple effect. You deliver your messages to the primary audience and they, in turn, share this information with others. To take advantage of this process, ask audience members to pass along your key messages so others can hear your ideas and understand your views.

- *Using handouts:* Secondary audiences always need to be considered if you plan to give handouts. Think about how someone who didn't attend the presentation will view the materials you plan to distribute.

- *Limiting leaks:* If you plan to present any confidential information, recognize the danger of including this information in a handout. Even if you don't put this information in a handout, you may still have trouble controlling who hears it.

II. WHAT DO THEY KNOW AND EXPECT?

The second question focuses on the audience's knowledge and their expectations.

What do they know about the topic?   Think about your audience's background and information needs. Since you want to avoid boring the experts or baffling the beginners, keep these points in mind:

- *Identify unfamiliar terms and jargon* before you start designing your presentation. What may be a common term to you may be an unknown concept to many in the audience. On the other hand, if the audience has a special vocabulary, you may want to learn and use their lingo during your presentation.

- *Consider how to handle the mixed backgrounds* in the room. You may find that the experts are more willing to listen to basic explanations if they see that most people in the room don't share their expertise. An informal poll at the start of the presentation may alert the audience to the mixed backgrounds in the room. As another option, you may be able to provide background material to audience members before the presentation. Be sure to pay special attention to the background and information needs of key decision makers. While you don't want to confuse anyone in the group, you certainly don't want to bore decision makers with information that seems too basic or data they don't care to see.

- *Look for ways to separate the basic messages* from more elaborate details. When you design your presentation, remember that everyone must be able to follow your basic points, but you may be able to keep the experts involved by referring to examples or issues that will interest them, while alerting others that a brief digression isn't central to your point.

What do they know about you?   Figure out what the audience already knows about you and then try to assess their views. Consider what they know about your competence and your character. For example: What do they know about your background? Do they consider you an expert? Will they trust you to be fair? By asking such questions, you can begin to assess your initial credibility, which is the credibility you have before you present. (Pages 32–33 have more information about credibility.)

What do they expect in terms of format? Find out what the audience expects in terms of room set up, formality level, timing, ground rules, and visual aids. Clearly, you don't want to waste time preparing a formal, one-hour presentation if your audience thinks you'll be delivering an informal, 15-minute talk. Similarly, if you plan to ask people to hold their questions until the end of your presentation, but the departmental norm is to ask questions throughout, realize that the audience may either resent or simply not follow your initial request. Never run the risk of irritating or inconveniencing the very same people you hope to persuade. Therefore, if you plan to go against the norm in terms of format expectations, be prepared to explain why you are engaging in the unexpected.

What do they expect in terms of culture? Every aspect of your strategy will be greatly influenced by the cultural context in which you are communicating. By "culture," we include the country, region, industry, organization, gender, ethnic group, and work group. Much of the material in this book is geared toward giving presentations in a Western business culture. If you are planning to give a presentation to people from another culture, get assistance from someone who knows that culture. Here are a few cross-cultural considerations to keep in mind (for more information, see the Munter article in the bibliography):

- *Cultural attitudes toward time:* You might want to take a different approach in a culture that is relaxed and relative about time than you would in a culture that is more precise about it.

- *Cultural attitudes toward whom to include:* You may need to include additional audience members depending on cultural expectations about rank, authority, and group definition.

- *Cultural differences in motivation:* You may find that different motivational techniques will work more effectively in different cultures. Although some cultures value material wealth and acquisition, others place greater value on work relationships, challenges, or status.

- *Cultural norms about communication medium:* Some cultures may routinely use standardized one-page memos while others prefer face-to-face hallway discussions. You might find different medium usage in a traditional organization versus a start-up venture.

III. WHAT DO THEY FEEL?

Remember, your audience's emotional level is just as important as their knowledge level. Many presenters mistakenly think that all business audiences are driven by facts and rationality alone. In truth, they may also be driven by their feelings about you or your message: they may experience positive emotions such as pride, excitement, and hope, or negative ones, such as anxiety, fear, or jealousy.

In addition to these feelings, consider their general emotional state. Is there anything about the current economic situation, the timing, or their morale that you should keep in mind? More specifically, analyze their interest level, bias, and attitude toward what you want them to do.

Are they interested?   Does your topic excite the audience or bore them? Is your message a high priority or a low one? Will they listen carefully to what you say or will they quickly tune you out?

- *High interest level:* If everyone's interest level will be high, you can get right to the point without taking much time to arouse their interest. If you are planning an informative talk, be sure to leave plenty of time for questions, because most groups want to discuss the topics that intrigue them.

- *Low or mixed interest level:* If, on the other hand, some members of the audience have a low interest level, use techniques to grab their attention and overcome their indifference. Many of the techniques described on page 27–33 can be used to motivate bored audience members. In addition, consider building interest by asking for audience participation and be sure to maintain that interest by keeping your presentation as short as possible. If you are delivering a sales presentation, try to act quickly on any attitude changes that occur as a result of your sales pitch; such changes may not be permanent with this type of audience.

What is their bias?   Consider their attitude toward you and your message. Are they likely to favor your ideas, be indifferent, or be opposed? What do they have to gain and what do they have to lose? Why might they say "yes"? And why might they say "no"?

- *Positive or neutral:* If their bias about your message is positive or neutral, reinforce their attitude by stating the benefits that accrue from your message.

- *Negative:* If they have a negative bias toward your message or recommendation, try to list all their possible objections and use the suggestions on pages 27–33 to help overcome them. In particular, focus on the ask-for-less appeal: (1) Limit your request to the smallest one possible, such as a pilot program rather than a full program. (2) Build off small agreements. For example, first get them to agree that there is a problem and then recommend a way to solve that problem. As another example, first state the ideas with which they will agree, knowing that if they are sold on the first few features, they will tend to sell themselves on the following ones as well. Finally, if their negative feelings are linked to you, see pages 32–33 for ways to improve your credibility.

Are you asking for a little or a lot?   Think about what you want the audience to do as a result of your presentation. Are you asking them to perform a task that will be time consuming, complicated, or difficult? Or, will it be fairly easy for them to comply with your requests? If you aren't clear about what you want from your audience, see pages 14 and 15, which explain how to set a presentation objective. Once you've created this objective, you'll be able to decide whether you are asking for a little or asking for a lot.

- *Asking for a little:* Even if you are asking very little of your audience, still point out the value of their effort—explain how it supports their beliefs or how it benefits them in some way.

- *Asking for a lot:* If what you are asking will be difficult or time-consuming for your audience, try one of these techniques: (1) Make the action as easy as possible. For example, provide a checklist of new procedures so they will be easy to follow. (2) Break the action down into the smallest possible request. For example, only ask for a signature to approve your idea and then arrange for someone else to take on the work of implementing it.

CHAPTER 2 OUTLINE

I. SET YOUR OBJECTIVE AND INTERACTION LEVEL.
  1. Determine your presentation objective.
  2. Decide on desired level of interaction.

II. CHOOSE THE APPROPRIATE MEDIUM.
  1. Should you make a presentation?
  2. Should you add another medium to your presentation?
  3. Should you decide against giving a presentation?

CHAPTER 2

Identifying Your Intent

In addition to thinking about what your audience wants and needs, part of your strategy involves analyzing what you want and need, that is, identifying your intent: (1) setting your objective and desired level of audience interaction and (2) choosing the appropriate medium (also known as "channel"), in other words, deciding when to make a presentation, when to hold a meeting, and so forth.

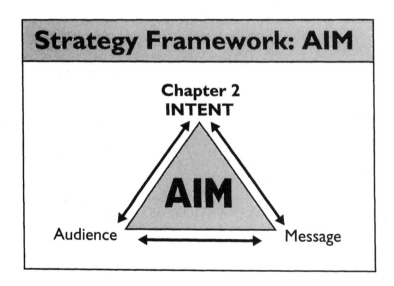

I. SET YOUR OBJECTIVE
AND INTERACTION LEVEL.

Step one in identifying your intent is to transform your general purpose into a clearly stated presentation objective. As part of this process,
consider how much audience interaction you'll want or need to have.

1. Determine your presentation objective.

Ineffective presenters often become so involved in gathering and analyzing data, designing their visuals, and worrying about delivery, that
they completely lose sight of what they are trying to accomplish. Avoid
such pitfalls by always writing a clear presentation objective as part of
your strategy.

Why?   A presentation objective will keep you focused. Furthermore,
after the presentation, it will provide the only true measure as to
whether your efforts were successful. An effective presentation is not
the result of beautiful visual aids or a flawless delivery; rather, an
effective presentation is one that accomplishes its objective. While
designing and delivering a presentation may be considered more of an
art than a science, the presentation objective offers concrete proof as
to whether your efforts were successful.

How?   A presentation objective defines precisely how you would
like your audience to respond to your presentation. Begin by jotting
down your general purpose. Then use the following process to set your
objective:

- Write the phrase "As a result of my presentation, the audience will . . ."
- Then, complete the presentation objective by identifying exactly what
  you want your audience to do, say, or know as a result of your talk.
- Next, critique your efforts. Make sure your objective is specific, mea-
  surable, and focused on the audience.
- Finally, use audience analysis insight to determine whether your objective is attainable and worthwhile.

PRESENTATION OBJECTIVES	
General Purpose	**Presentation Objective**
Explain departmental results	As a result of my presentation, people in the department will have a monthly breakdown of our revenues and expenses and be aware of where we hit and missed our previous projections.
Share new record-keeping procedures	As a result of my presentation, the staff will (1) receive a guidebook on how to log their consulting time, (2) review examples of right and wrong ways to complete the logs, and (3) learn of the new 4 p.m. deadline for weekly submissions.
Generate financing for a new venture	As a result of my presentation, at least one member of the audience will agree to read my business plan and schedule a follow-up meeting with our senior management team.
Recommend a vendor	As a result of my presentation, the purchasing group will agree to split our next order, awarding a trial order to vendor X, so that we may compare quality and delivery time between vendors.

2. Decide on desired level of interaction.

Given your presentation objective, determine how much audience interaction you need to best accomplish that objective. To do so, think about the tradeoff between your control of the content versus the amount of audience interaction, as illustrated on the figure below.

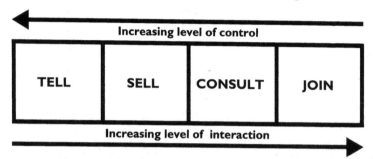

Tell presentations   In a tell presentation, you are trying to inform or explain. In these cases, you already have the information you need and you are not relying on an interactive session with the audience to gain information. Examples of tell presentations include reporting or updating on a project, explaining how something works, or announcing a company policy.

Sell presentations   In a sell presentation, you are seeking to persuade; you may be selling an idea or product or changing opinions or behaviors. For example, perhaps you want the audience to authorize a purchase, provide you with venture capital, or select your bid. Be aware that in many sell presentations, you will have to involve your audience emotionally, not just intellectually.

Consult/join interactions   In a consult/join interaction, you want to learn from the audience. You lack sufficient information; or you need to understand others' opinions or ideas; or you need to involve your audience, coming up with ideas collaboratively. For example, you might want your customers to share their opinions about a current product or service, or your staff to offer suggestions on team goals for the year. In a "consult" style, you control the content somewhat (such as offering three alternatives for discussion); in a "join" style, you do not control the content (such as initiating a brainstorming session).

II. CHOOSE THE APPROPRIATE MEDIUM.

Based on the tradeoffs you have just considered, choose the appropriate medium (also known as "channel"): that is, make a presentation, hold a meeting, or write.

1. Should you make a presentation?

Weigh the advantages and disadvantages of presentations as a medium of communication.

Advantages   Make a presentation when you want to: (1) ensure that a specified audience all hear and see the same information at the same time; (2) receive immediate and interactive response, from observing nonverbal reactions around the room and from answering questions; (3) use more than just words, since presentations include nonverbal and visual elements, without technological distortions; and (4) as in all face-to-face channels, build relationships.

Disadvantages   Remember, however, the disadvantages of presentations. They (1) are less interactive than meetings; (2) are less private and confidential than writing or one-to-one channels; (3) do not provide any permanent and accessible record; (4) do not allow for as much detail as writing because listeners cannot retain all the information they hear; and (5) are less precise than writing because speakers cannot edit what they say.

2. Should you add another medium to your presentation?

You also might consider adding another medium in conjunction with a presentation.

Add handouts?   If you need to discuss complex information, you might hand out a spreadsheet or detailed handout at the point in your presentation when you are discussing those numbers—instead of displaying the spreadsheet or handout in their microscopic type, along with your other slides.

Use a flipbook?   An increasingly prevalent method that combines media is that of using a flipbook made up of printed copy of your slides. These flipbooks can be used either:

- *During the presentation:* Sometimes, presenters use flipbooks as their primary visual aid throughout the presentation; the speaker and the audience members look at the hard copy together.
- *Before or after the presentation:* Other times, presenters use an expanded flipbook—consisting of copies of the visual aids plus supporting text and background data—as a pre- or post-presentation report.

Add some interaction (Q&A)?   Most presentations become somewhat more interactive through the use of questions and answers. Q&A can range from questions of understanding to questions of opinion. Think about how you want to handle questions and answers. (See pages 47–51 for more information on how to do so.)

Add an additional medium before or after your presentation?   If your presentation objective is too large to be accomplished with a single presentation, you may need to combine several efforts to achieve the desired outcome. For example, to provide background information, you may choose to phone several members of the audience before the presentation or you may decide to distribute a pre-presentation report to the entire group. On the other hand, you may elect to think of your presentation as a first step, following it up with other communication efforts that you will be able to arrange as a result of your presentation.

Present by videoconference?   Choose to present by videoconference when (1) the participants are in different places, but you want to communicate with them all at the same time; (2) you want to save on travel time and expenses; or (3) you want to record the presentation for future use or distribution. On the other hand, videoconferences (1) are usually not as effective as face-to-face presentations when you need to establish relationships; (2) lack the richest nonverbal cues, such as proximity and touch; (3) tend to be dominated by certain audience members—speaking in longer bursts than they do face-to-face; (4) may involve significant setup time and costs.

Present by conference call?   Conference calls have the same advantages of videoconferencing, plus they may be faster to set up and use more easily accessible equipment. Their disadvantages are that they (1) lack body language—making it harder to interact and to know who is going to speak next, and (2) lack text or visuals—making it harder to communicate a great deal of detailed or complex information.

3. Should you decide against giving a presentation?

Sometimes your best strategy may be to decide not to make a presentation and to use another medium instead.

Should you call a meeting instead? By "meeting," we mean an interactive group discussion, as opposed to a presentation, in which one speaker dominates the discussion. In a consult/join meeting, you can (1) gather information or generate ideas from other people; (2) make a group decision or reach consensus, or (3) build commitment through group empowerment or intragroup relationships. However, with a meeting, you (1) do not control the message content, (2) do not control the group decision, and (3) can waste time if the meeting is not facilitated properly.

Should you write instead? Don't waste people's time in a meeting or a presentation when you do not need interaction—such as for routine announcements, clarifications, or confirmation. People can read much faster than they can hear. Therefore, write when you want to have (1) a permanent and accessible record; (2) a private communication; (3) precise wording and grammar, because you can edit; or (4) a great deal of detail, because readers can assimilate more detail than listeners can. If you write, however, you may have (1) no control over if or when the message is received; (2) a delayed response, if any; (3) no nonverbal communication; or (4) a possible lack of flexibility and too much rigidity.

Should you speak to one individual instead? Do you really need to present to a group of people—or actually just one or two? Speak to an individual, not to a group, when you want to (1) get individual feedback or response, (2) build your individual relationship or rapport, or (3) deal with a sensitive or negative issue—too sensitive or negative to discuss in a group. Remember, however, the disadvantages of speaking to one person only. (1) It may make those with whom you do not speak feel excluded. (2) If you speak with more than one person separately, they will each hear slightly different information at different times.

CHAPTER 3 OUTLINE

I. EMPHASIZE KEY IDEAS.
 1. Use techniques to improve recall.
 2. Highlight important messages.

II. BE PERSUASIVE.
 1. **A** = Appeals that overcome audience objections
 2. **B** = Benefit statements that explain "what's in it for them"
 3. **C** = Credibility appeals that focus on the speaker

CHAPTER 3

Making Your Message Memorable

So far, we have looked at the first two components of presentation strategy, analyzing your audience and identifying your intent. This chapter explains the third strategic component, making your message memorable. To do so, use the techniques from this chapter to (1) emphasize your key ideas and (2) become persuasive.

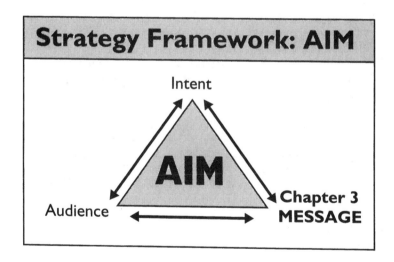

I. EMPHASIZE KEY IDEAS.

While your audience may try to listen to all your data, examples, facts, and opinions, in reality, they can only take in and recall a small portion of what you say. Therefore, to make your message memorable, you need to know how to emphasize key ideas.

1. Use techniques to improve recall.

Understand the importance of the beginning and the end. When you begin your presentation, audience attention tends to be high, but as you continue to talk, attention may wander. Some people tune in and out; others fall prey to long bouts of daydreaming. Nevertheless, when you say the words "finally" or "in conclusion," most of them perk up. They listen intently, hoping to find out what they may have missed along the way.

Not surprisingly, how your audience listens to your presentation will also affect what they remember. The Audience Memory Curve, shown below, is a graphic representation of a well-known principle: people tend to recall what they hear or see at the beginning and end of a presentation more than what appears in the middle. Therefore, the two most emphatic locations for your key ideas are first or last (or both).

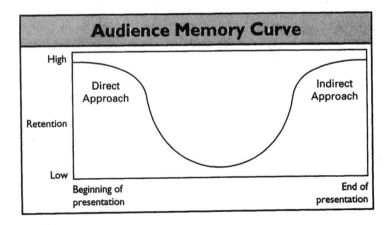

State your main idea first or last.   The Audience Memory Curve also points out the difference between the direct and indirect approach.

- *Direct approach:* The direct approach is sometimes called the "bottom-line-approach" because it emphasizes the bottom line during the opening of the presentation. When your audience knows your recommendation or your conclusions up front, they have an easier time following your supporting ideas.

- *Indirect approach:* By contrast, the indirect approach saves the recommendation or the conclusions for the end of the presentation. Therefore, this approach is like a mystery story; it takes a long time for the audience to determine where all the evidence is leading.

Use a direct approach whenever possible.

- *It improves comprehension:* People assimilate content more easily when they know the conclusions first. Withholding your conclusions for the end is fine for mystery readers, but not for busy executives who may resent every minute they spend trying to figure out what you're attempting to say.

- *It's audience-focused:* The direct approach emphasizes the results of the analysis. By contrast, a communicator-focused approach simply follows the process you used to conduct your analysis. Most audiences care less about you and your process than they do about the results.

- *It saves time:* When you use the direct approach, the audience understands your message quickly.

Because the direct approach is easier and faster to follow, you should use it as much as possible in Anglo-American business situations, probably about 90% of the time. It's the best option for all non-sensitive messages. It can also be used for sensitive or emotional messages if the audience has a positive bias, if they are results-oriented, or if your credibility is particularly high.

Use the indirect approach with caution.   Since the indirect approach is harder to follow and takes longer to understand, use it with care. In some situations, it may prevent the audience from disagreeing with you right away, soften their resistance to an unpopular idea, or increase their tendency to see you as fair-minded. Nevertheless, use this approach only when certain constraints require you to do so:

- *Audience and message constraints:* You have a sensitive message with emotional overtones, a negatively-biased audience, and low credibility. Or, you have an analysis-oriented key decision maker who insists upon it.

- *Cultural constraints:* You are presenting in another culture where the direct approach would be viewed as inappropriate or pushy.

Chunk information. Another way to help people recall key ideas is to limit the number you use. Cognitive psychologists have shown that people cannot easily comprehend and remember more than five to seven items. This finding does not mean that you should stand up, make five points, and then sit down. Rather, it explains why you need to learn how to make your message memorable.

Packaging information into sections, or "chunking" it, dramatically improves recall. Therefore, you may be able to cover dozens of topics in your presentation, if you can find ways to categorize them. Probably, some are related to others; if so, perhaps they can be chunked into three or four ideas and then presented as the three or four major sections of your presentation.

One benefit of chunking information is that by doing so, you change the look of the Audience Memory Curve. Instead of having one long curve with a big dip, you create several "mini-memory" curves, each with its own dip and peaks. In essence, chunking your ideas enables you to create even more emphatic locations—or peaks—for your key ideas.

Include a preview. A preview is a brief statement that provides an overview of how you plan to structure your talk. Previews are very important for your audience, because listeners, unlike readers, can't flip back and see what they've just missed. Instead, they have to rely on what you've previously told them about the presentation's structure. Therefore, early in your presentation, be sure to provide a preview that tells people how you plan to organize your talk. (See page 44.)

2. Highlight important messages.

What else can you do to keep your audience from nodding off during the middle part of your presentation? Choose from among the following six techniques to highlight important messages.

Repetition   Information that is repeated tends to get noticed. Therefore, one way to emphasize a key message is through repetition. For example, you might introduce each section of your presentation and then summarize that section before moving to the next one; by doing so, the audience will hear the major point at least three times. However, try to vary the way you repeat key messages to prevent the repetition from being monotonous. Also try not to repeat insignificant information.

Flagging   This technique is direct and easy to use. You simply "flag" (or draw attention to) important points by saying something such as "If you remember only one thing I tell you today, remember . . ." or "Here's the most important point I want to make . . ."—the business equivalent of a professor saying "This material is going to be on the final exam." No matter which words or phrases you select, they should be ones that tell the audience an important message is coming up next.

The unexpected   ("the Von Restorff effect") People tend to remember that which is different or unexpected—called "the Von Restorff effect" after the psychologist who researched this phenomenon. By using a surprise or an attention-getting change in your presentation, you can focus the audience's attention on a key point that would otherwise be lost—for example, suddenly adding humor, telling a surprising story, dramatically changing your delivery style, showing an attention-grabbing photograph or video clip, or altering the pace of your presentation in an unexpected way. As with other highlighting techniques, the more you repeat this technique, the less emphasis each use will have. Also be aware that an attention-getting device that is seen as too gimmicky may serve to damage your credibility and, at the same time, make the damaging moment very memorable.

Mnemonics   Mnemonic devices—aids to help the memory—can also be used to highlight messages. For example, we used the mnemonic "AIM" in the first three chapters to stress that strategy involves Analyzing the audience, Identifying your intent, and Making your message memorable. Such devices are especially useful if you want to emphasize five or more categories.

Audience involvement   People tend to drift off as they listen; therefore, to make something stand out, you may need to increase your audience's involvement, having them do more than just listen. You may want to ask a single question or use a question and answer session to increase involvement. Sometimes, presenters use simulations, demonstrations, and discussions to highlight messages.

Visual reinforcement   During a presentation, the presenter is the most important visual; nevertheless, well-designed and properly positioned visuals can make a presentation more effective. If audiences see an important message while they listen to it, they are more likely to recall that message. In addition, if a speaker uses only one visual, that message will stand out more than if 50 visuals are used. Or if one visual is different than others—perhaps a photograph as opposed to 20 text visuals—then the unusual visual will likely capture their attention. (See pages 53–81 for more on visual aids.)

II. BE PERSUASIVE.

So far, we have looked at ways to make your message memorable through techniques involving your message's ideas. The following section deals with another way to make your message memorable— by persuading your audience. (A third set of techniques, structuring the presentation, is covered on pages 43–46.)

Persuasion is a complex topic, but in an effort to streamline it for you, here are some ABCs for persuasive presentations. They include: (1) **A** = Appeals that can overcome audience objections; (2) **B** = Benefit statements that explain "what's in it for them"; and (3) **C** = Credibility-based techniques that focus more on the speaker's credibility than on the audience's benefits.

1. A = Appeals to overcome audience objections

Your audience analysis may uncover possible objections to your topic or recommendations. Common objections about a recommendation tend to be about cost, timing, risk, change, effort, or the desirability of other options. If you know these potential objections in advance, you can figure out ways to overcome them, either in your talk or during Q&A. Several of the following appeals may prove useful.

Bottom-line appeals   If you think your audience may object based on cost or risks, try using number-based arguments that present comparative data, trends, and forecasts. Most business audiences appreciate, are comfortable with, and may be swayed by such quantitative appeals. However, because these audiences tend to be numerically sophisticated, they are likely to see through and reject such techniques as taking statistics out of context, making faulty comparisons, forecasting trends too extravagantly, or using unreliable sources. Therefore, to use numbers persuasively, you will need to be aware of the information behind the numbers and be prepared to defend them.

Benchmarking or bandwagon appeals   If you think the audience's objections might be assuaged by knowing what others are doing, as often happens in situations involving change or uncertainty, try using benchmarking/bandwagon appeals. For example, if the head of Human

Resources hears that four out of five major competitors have implemented a casual dress code, then she might be more likely to agree to a policy she once viewed as unprofessional. When trying to get someone to follow the lead, choose a pool of others that the audience will consider both appealing and similar. As communication expert JoAnne Yates points out, "although the fact that 'everyone else is doing it' may not be a very good logical argument, it nevertheless influences some people."

Ask for less   (also known as the "foot-in-the-door technique" or "initial concession technique") Sometimes, your communication objective will be so expansive that the audience will object to its scope, whether their concern is "it's just too expensive," or "it will drain other resources if we try to implement it." In these cases, consider asking for only a small part of what you really want. Suggest a pilot program, recommend a trial purchase, or sign up volunteers for a fact-finding committee. Any of these small steps is equivalent to getting your foot in the door. Once people have given you an initial commitment, you will have an easier time getting many of them to accept your future appeals. To make the small step even more powerful, get people to voice their agreement publicly or in writing. As social psychologist Robert Cialdini explains, most people want to be viewed as "consistent" and will continue to back efforts they have publicly and actively supported.

Ask for more   (also known as the "door-in-the-face technique" or "reciprocal concessions technique") This tactic is the opposite of the previous one. If you think your audience will object to what you hope to accomplish, the door-in-the-face strategy has you begin by asking for far more than you really want. After the audience objects to your overwhelming request, you find out whether they are willing to accept part of it. After all, if you are willing to lessen your demands, it seems only fair that they should compromise, too. Fund raisers sometimes use this approach, initially asking for a $50,000 donation, but later requesting the more reasonable sum of $500. Clearly, there is a danger in playing the back-and-forth game of reciprocal concessions, which is a positional bargaining technique—if the audience feels no need to work with you, they may simply slam the door.

Limited opportunity appeals   When timing is one of the objections, presenters can point to a "small window of opportunity" or encourage people to "buy now while supplies last." Deadlines sometimes move people to act without all the information they would normally seek. Similarly, the laws of supply and demand kick in when people learn that something will soon be scarce; the inability to acquire something in the future may make it appear more valuable today.

2. B = Benefit statements that explain "what's in it for them"

One of the most common concepts taught in sales training involves turning a feature into a benefit. These lessons can be applied to persuasive presentations. The acronym "WIIFM" means "what's in it for me?" Most audiences are eagerly waiting for you to answer this question with a benefit statement.

There are three steps to creating benefit statements. First, identify all the features of an idea or a product. Second, put those features through an audience filter to determine which ones benefit your audience. Finally, generate a benefit statement that clearly and specifically explains what's in it for them.

Step 1: Identify features. All ideas, products, and services have many, many features. Features are value free. They are simply facts about the item or idea you are selling. Consider the book you are reading. Here are some of its features: two authors, descriptive headings, six chapters, tips on how to design charts, chapter outlines, a bibliography, and so on. Some of these features could be turned into a benefit statement for an audience. Others may have little or no value to that same audience.

Identifying the features of an idea tends to be harder than generating features related to a concrete item such as this book. Nevertheless, try to identify the basic facts behind your ideas. You may discover that your recommendation to move corporate headquarters: "affects the commute of 750 people," "has two phases," "could begin this year," "includes building a new gym," "involves buying rather than leasing," and "will leave 50 undeveloped acres."

Step 2: Apply an audience filter. After you've identified as many features as possible, examine them from the audience's perspective. You may discover that some of your features will actually be objections. For example, while some members of senior management may be thrilled to have a new employee gym, others may consider it frivolous. Think carefully how people in the audience will respond to each feature. Focus on those that have a positive effect and will be important to the group. You may also want to filter in the reaction of people in the secondary audience before you develop specific statements.

Step 3: Create a targeted benefit statement. Benefit statements clearly explain "what's in it for them." The statements may relate to tangible benefits such as profits, stock options, or an employee gym. They may also involve on-the-job benefits, saving people time, simplifying a complex process, improving morale, or solving a work-related problem. Sometimes, simply noting how the feature leads to a general benefit is enough. At other times, you need to go to this next level, creating a statement that makes a strong impression on the key decision maker and the rest of the audience.

Returning to the example about moving a company's headquarters, the table below shows how to take a feature and turn it into a targeted benefit statement.

TURNING A FEATURE INTO A BENEFIT		
Step 1	**Step 2**	**Step 3**
Identify the feature	**Apply an audience filter**	**Create a targeted benefit statement**
The plan includes a new gym	For an audience who **wants to reduce costs**	We'll qualify for lower health-care fees if we have an on-site fitness facility.
	For an audience who **cares about employee relations**	We can mention the new gym at the next employee meeting as an example of what's being done to address work-life balance issues.
	For an audience who **feels stressed**	Employees can take stress-reducing yoga classes either over the lunch hour or after work.

3. C = Credibility appeals that focus on the speaker

Another way to be persuasive is based on your audience's opinion of you—that is, your credibility. Think first about the initial credibility you have with the audience before they hear your opening remarks. Which of the following kinds of credibility do you already have—and how might you use them? For example, should you stress your rank, track record, or expertise? Then, think about how you can enhance your credibility. For example, what should you include in your introduction? Or how might you associate yourself with someone the audience respects?

Remember, however, that your credibility will vary dramatically depending on each different audience you address. Below, we present various techniques to enhance your credibility. From among them, choose the ones that will work with your specific audience.

Résumé credibility   Some forms of credibility are based on traits that might be found on your résumé.

- *Authoritative or rank* appeals rely on hierarchical power. For some audiences, impressive titles, an affiliation with a prestigious institution, or even symbols of power and influence can serve to enhance your credibility. If you do not have this kind of credibility, you may choose to acquire it by associating yourself with a high-ranking person—such as having her or him introduce your presentation or write a cover letter announcing it.

- *Expertise* appeals are based on your experience or knowledge of the topic. For some audiences, you might choose to emphasize your educational or experiential background. Or, if your audience does not view you as an expert, you might cite expert sources the audience finds credible.

Character credibility   Other types of credibility are based more on your audience's perception of your character.

- *Similarity:* Audiences tend to like people who are similar to themselves, whether that similarity is reflected in common interests and backgrounds or in a familiar speaking style. Sometimes, you may wish to enhance your credibility by mentioning mutual experiences or using familiar jargon.

- *Common ground:* Another powerful way to enhance your credibility is to establish a common ground with your audience—emphasizing the values, ideas, problems, or needs you share.

- *Positive association:* Audiences tend to like speakers who deliver good news. Therefore, many audiences respond well to speakers who say complementary things about them. On the other hand, when speakers are associated with bad news or unpleasant situations, their credibility often suffers.

- *Attractiveness:* Speakers who present an attractive image may find that people assign other positive traits to them as well.

- *Goodwill:* People generally feel obliged to reciprocate positive actions with other positive actions. Credibility experts French and Raven refer to this as establishing "goodwill." Therefore, if you have done favors for audience members—lent them a hand, supported them in the past, or given them gifts—they may feel obligated to return the favor by going along with your request. Another aspect of goodwill credibility involves trustworthiness. If the audience views you as fair, you can maintain their trust by offering a balanced evaluation of your proposal and acknowledging any potential conflict of interest.

PART II

Implementation Framework

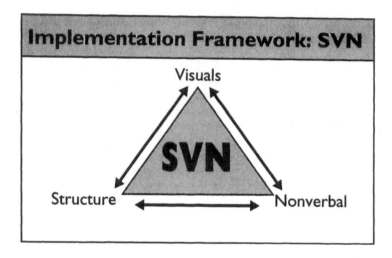

PART II

Presentation Implementation

W hat you have decided about your strategy—who will be in your audience, how interactive you want to be, how you can be persuasive—will ultimately drive the implementation concerns covered in the second part of this book.

Once again in Part II, we have provided a mnemonic device, illustrated on the facing page, for remembering the three components of presentation implementation.

- **S** stands for "structure"—what you say during your presentation (Chapter 4)
- **V** stands for "visuals"—what your audience sees during your presentation (Chapter 5)
- **N** stands for "nonverbal delivery"—how you look and sound to your audience (Chapter 6)

As you can see from the SVN framework illustration at left, the three components do not necessarily occur in lockstep order. The arrows show how all three of them interact. For example, your structure will affect your visual aids design and your choice of visual aids will affect your nonverbal delivery.

CHAPTER 4 OUTLINE

I. RESEARCH AND ORGANIZE YOUR CONTENT.
   1. Collect the information.
   2. Organize the information.

II. DECIDE WHAT TO SAY.
   1. What to say during a tell/sell presentation
   2. What to say during question-and-answer sessions

CHAPTER 4

Structuring Your Presentation

In this chapter, we consider the structural aspects of a presentation—that is, how you collect, focus, and order what you'll say. Structuring a presentation involves two sets of techniques: (1) how to research and organize your content, and (2) how to decide what to say—in both tell/sell presentations and question-and-answer sessions.

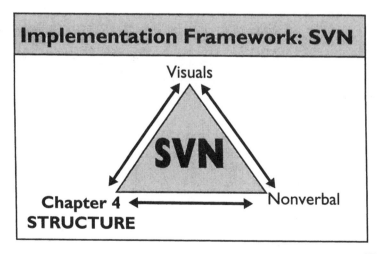

I. RESEARCH AND ORGANIZE YOUR CONTENT.

An effective presentation structure is based on effective information therefore, use the following guidelines as you consider the content of your presentation.

1. Collect the information.

Here is a process to help you gather and focus information:

- *Determine what you already know about the topic.* Frequently speakers are already very knowledgeable about the presentation topic. In tell presentations, the speaker may be an expert. Similarly, in sell presentations, the speaker may be a known advocate for the product or cause. Nevertheless, even in these cases, you should still gather all the information in your head and in your files to begin the process.

- *Conduct the necessary research to add to your knowledge.* Jot down your general ideas; gather materials from articles and reports; analyze data; access information from the web or databases; call people; if you prefer working with others, discuss what you may be talking about with someone else.

- *Do a data dump* of all the information you now have.

- *Apply two filters to the data dump.* Filter through the data dump of information based on (1) your analysis of audience knowledge, expectations, and feelings (as explained on pages 6–11), and (2) your presentation objective (as explained on pages 14–15). Some presenters find it helpful to post a note on their wall reminding them of their audience members and presentation objective as they work through the process of designing their presentation.

- *Adjust audience or objective if necessary.* You may find that you want to add or subtract people from your audience. Or you may find you need to adjust your objective; if so, write a new one and keep it in mind as you continue.

- *Conduct additional research if necessary.* Find out more about the topic if necessary for your audience or your objective.

2. Organize the information.

To order all the information you collect, find a method for grouping similar ideas. In other words, develop an "organizational blueprint" for your presentation.

What the different methods are   If using a traditional outline—with Roman numerals, capital letters, and so forth—doesn't help you organize your ideas, try one of the following useful methods:

- *Idea charts (pyramid-shaped):* (1) List your "data dump" of ideas; (2) organize ideas into groups; (3) label each group. Idea charts look like a pyramid, with the main idea at the top and subordinate points beneath.

- *Mind maps (circular):* (1) Write your presentation objective in a circle in the middle of the page; (2) then, connect your subordinate points like spokes around the circle—using words, phrases, images, dotted lines, and so forth to represent and connect points. Mind maps can include pictures and other visual images.

- *Storyboards (series of slides):* (1) Start with a series of blank boxes, to represent your visual aids; (2) sketch in key messages and images, starting with an agenda slide and then adding sketches of possible backup slides.

- *Personalized methods:* Use a combination of the above methods or adopt others that may involve using index cards, sticky notes, or computer software.

The following pages show examples of an idea chart, a mind map, and a storyboard. For further details, refer to the Buzon book on mind mapping or the Minto book on the pyramid principal, both in the bibliography.

Organizing with an Idea Chart

"Data clump of ideas"

Eliminate product X.

Provide *pro forma* statements.

Redefine departmental responsibilities.

Decrease capital expenditures.

Expand marketing division.

Concentrate on product Y.

Renegotiate short-term liability.

Idea chart of ideas

```
                          Recommendations
              ┌───────────────────┼───────────────────┐
          Product Mix          Finiancial          Organizational
          ┌────┴────┐       ┌──────┼──────┐        ┌──────┴──────┐
```

| Eliminate product x. | Concentrate on product y. | Provide *pro forma* statements. | Decrease capital expenditures | Renegotiate short-term liability. | Redefine departmental responsibilities. | Expand marketing department. |

Organizing with a Mind Map

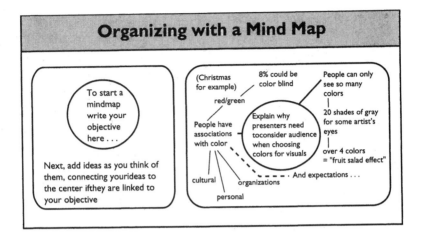

To start a mindmap write your objective here . . .

Next, add ideas as you think of them, connecting yourideas to the center ifthey are linked to your objective

(Christmas for example)
red/green

8% could be color blind

People can only see so many colors

People have associations with color

Explain why presenters need toconsider audience when choosing colors for visuals

20 shades of gray for some artist's eyes

over 4 colors = "fruit salad effect"

cultural

organizations

And expectations . . .

personal

Organizing with a Storyboard

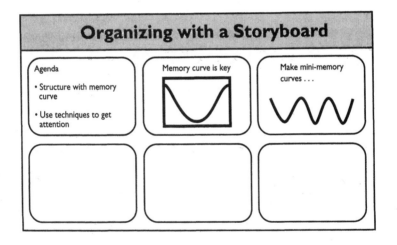

Agenda

• Structure with memory curve

• Use techniques to get attention

Memory curve is key

Make mini-memory curves . . .

How to choose a method   To choose the method that will work best for you, consider what kind of thinker you tend to be.

* *Linear thinkers:* If you are a highly structured thinker, then idea charts or traditional outlining methods will likely work best for you.

* *Random thinkers:* If you like to go off on tangents and easily find connections between ideas, then outlines may seem restrictive to you. Consider using a mind map to collect, focus, and order the content of your talk.

* *Visual thinkers:* Generally, people who readily recall images prefer visual organizational methods, such as mind mapping or storyboarding. Visual thinkers who prefer a random approach, tend to like mind mapping, whereas those who prefer a sequential approach often find storyboarding an effective ordering method.

How to choose in teams   Recognizing different ordering preferences is especially important when working on a team presentation. While the various ordering methods may be complementary, someone who likes to outline will most likely be baffled by a group mind-mapping session. Similarly, someone who likes to sketch images may feel stifled by a group that needs to begin with a presentation outline.

II. DECIDE WHAT TO SAY.

Once you have researched and organized your material, it's time to figure out how to structure that material into what you'll actually say during your presentation and your question-and-answer session.

I. What to say during a tell/sell presentation

Presentation structure is somewhat different than the more familiar structure we use for writing. Because listeners, unlike readers, have had a time and a place imposed on them and cannot glance back and forth at your main points, all presentations need (1) an opening, (2) a preview (or topic outline), (3) clearly delineated main points, and (4) a strong closing.

The four elements of the structure appear in the order listed above when you actually deliver the presentation; however, you do not need to compose them in that order. Some people like to begin by creating the closing first, ensuring that it will accomplish the presentation objective. Others prefer a more chronological approach, beginning with a possible preview, working through the body, and finishing with the closing. Yet others revisit the preview last, to make sure it parallels the main points.

Prepare an effective opening.   The opening is crucial to build your credibility, audience interest, and audience understanding.

- *Set the stage.* The opening sets the stage; it introduces you and your presentation. If you are unknown to anyone in the audience, you may need to use the opening to introduce yourself and establish your credibility. If your topic is not an audience favorite, you may need to explain it and show how it relates to the audience.

- *"Grab" their attention.* Often, your audience has other things on their minds or is not especially interested in your topic, so you may need to use what many experts call a "grabber" to arouse their interest. Some common grabbers include: asking a question; making a promise of what your presentation will deliver; describing a vivid image; sharing a startling story, example, or statistic; or referring to audience benefits (as explained on pages 30–31.) The most overused grabbers include reading quotations or reciting definitions, which, since they are often overused or simply not very interesting, frequently fail to grab much attention.

- *Use humor with caution.* Humor can be an effective grabber; however, use it only if it fits your personality and style, if it is appropriate for every member of the audience, and if it relates to the topic or occasion. Never use humor that might make anyone feel left out, put down, or trivialized.

- *State your recommendation.* In most sell presentations, your recommendation will also appear in the opening. In such cases, you are opting to use what is known as a "direct" structure, as we discussed on page 23.

Include a preview.   All presentations need a preview (also called an agenda or a table of contents) that tells the audience how the upcoming talk will be structured. For example, the preview might sound like this: "In the next 20 minutes, I want to go over two topics—first, I want to describe our work flow problems in the Houston and Cleveland offices; second, I want to discuss the four alternatives we have in dealing with these problems."

The preview gives the audience the outline of what you'll be saying, or in the words of Mark Twain, the preview tells them what you're going to tell them. Because it is such an important part of the presentation, ideally, the preview will also be visible on a visual aid or handout.

State your main points clearly.   On page 24, we discussed the importance of chunking information into two to five sections, which form the body of the presentation. When you present material orally, you need to state those main points explicitly, using the following techniques. These techniques may feel like "overkill" to an inexperienced speaker, but they are absolutely necessary for the audience because they process information differently through their ears than they do through their eyes (for listening, they need more repetition).

- *Organizational patterns:* Your main points may be organized in dozens of ways, but some common ones include: (1) *Key points:* point one/point two/point three; (2) *Key questions:* what I'm recommending/why we need it/how we can implement it; (3) *Problem/solution:* explanation of the problem/possible ways to solve it.

- *Internal summaries:* No matter how you choose to organize the body, be sure you provide internal summaries. Here is an example of an internal summary, followed by an explicit transition to the next section:

  "Now that we have looked at the three elements of the marketing plan—modifying the promotion program, increasing direct mail, and eliminating the coupon program—let's turn to the financial implications of the plan."

- *Explicit transitions:* In the example above, you can see that the transitions are long and very descriptive. They need to be. Your listeners lose track of where you are, and since they are not reading your message, they can't flip back a few pages to catch up. By using such detailed transitions, you enable daydreamers to rejoin the presentation and remind others that you are working through the structure you described during the preview.

Prepare an effective closing. Another memorable part of the presentation, the closing should always be more that a brief "thank you." The closing needs to be linked to the presentation objective—what you want the audience to know, do, or say as a result of the presentation. Nevertheless, depending on the situation, the closing can take many forms.

- *Tell closings:* In a tell presentation, the closing should summarize key messages or remind the audience of your objective.
- *Sell closings:* In a sell presentation, the closing should close the sale. For example, you might close by asking the key decision makers for an order or by requesting authorization to implement your recommendation. Or you might collect the names of those who have volunteered to join your efforts. In yet another case, you might close after the presentation, in a private conversation.

The figure on the following page illustrates a common presentation structure for both a tell and a sell presentation. In tell presentations, your opening might include your presentation objective and a preview, while the closing might be a summary. In sell presentations, your recommendation and preview usually come first; your "call to action" comes at the end.

Common Tell Structure

Tell Opening

| Introduction |
| Preview |

Sample Body

Point 1	Summary/Transition
Point 2	Summary/Transition
Point 3	Summary/Transition

Tell Closing

| Summary |

Common Sell Structure

Sell Opening

| Introduction |
| Recommendation |
| Preview |

Sample Body

Reason 1	Summary/Transition
Reason 2	Summary/Transition
Reason 3	Summary/Transition

Sell Closing

| Action steps |

2. What to say during question-and-answer sessions

Most presentations involve interaction between the speaker and the audience in the form of questions and answers (Q&A). Dealing effectively with questions involves the following decisions, preparation, and skills.

Deciding when to take questions Well before the presentation, think about when you want to take questions. Then, be sure to inform your audience at the beginning of the presentation. Say, for example, "Please feel free to ask questions as they come up," or "Please hold all your questions until the end of the presentation," or "Feel free to interrupt with questions of understanding or clarification, but since we have only an hour together, please hold questions of debate or discussion until the end."

Usually, audience and cultural expectations are fairly clear: the current trend in most Anglo-American business presentations is to include questions during the presentation; sometimes, however, the norm is a Q&A period at the end of the presentation. If the choice is up to you, think about the following advantages and disadvantages.

- *Questions after the presentation:* If you take questions after the presentation, you will maintain control of the schedule and the flow of information. However, you risk (1) losing your audience's attention and perhaps even comprehension if they cannot ask their questions as they occur, and (2) placing yourself in an awkward position if important audience members interrupt with questions after you've asked them not to. Since audiences tend to remember more material from the beginning and end of a presentation, having Q&A at the end of your talk places undue emphasis on the question period. To alleviate this problem, leave time for a final closing after taking questions.

- *Questions during the presentation:* If you take questions during the presentation, the questions will be more meaningful to the questioner, the feedback will be more immediate, and your audience may listen more actively. However, questions during the presentation can upset your schedule and waste time. To alleviate these problems, (1) allow enough time for questions and (2) control digressions.

Preparing for questions From the time you begin your audience analysis, think about possible questions.

- *Anticipate what the questions will be.* Bring along extra information, perhaps even extra visual aids, to answer such questions if they come up. Another way to anticipate questions is to ask a colleague to play devil's advocate during your rehearsal.

- *Prepare for frequently asked questions* relating to (1) value ("Are you sure we really need this?"), (2) cost ("Can't we do it for less?"), (3) alternatives ("What happens if we don't do anything?"), (4) action ("How will you implement it?"), (5) details ("Are those the most recent numbers?"), (6) obstacles ("How will you motivate them to accept this change?"), (7) risk ("So what's the downside?"), and (8) timing ("Can't we put it off until next quarter?")

- *Develop a positive attitude.* Avoid a defensive attitude; instead, think of it as a compliment if your listeners are interested enough to ask questions for clarification, amplification, or justification.

Using effective listening skills   Author Robert Bolton breaks listening skills into clusters of behaviors that can be termed "attending," "encouraging," and "following" skills.

- *Attending skills:* Together, these nonverbal skills create the look of good listening. (1) Maintain a posture of involvement by directly facing the audience, keeping your arms and hands out of the way, looking toward the questioner, and avoiding distracting gestures, (such as picking up your notes, rubbing your shoulder, or clicking a pen). Let your posture and stillness signal that you want to hear the question. (2) Use effective eye contact. Observe the questioner's whole face to pick up the nonverbal cues that may be part of the question. (3) Create an environment suitable for listening. Move to the side of the podium or the front of the table, closing the distance between you and your audience; ask everyone to direct their attention to the questioner so side conversations don't distract; and turn off projectors and noisy fans.

- *Encouraging skills:* These skills set the tone, encouraging people to make comments and share their views. (1) Wait for their questions. After asking for questions, give people at least 10 to 15 seconds to think. Don't say anything while you wait. (2) Ask open-ended questions that cannot be easily answered "yes" or "no." If your question starts with the words "Can you" or "Do you," then it can be answered with a single word such as "Yes." On the other hand, if you begin by saying "What do you . . ." or "Tell me about . . ." then your opening is more likely to yield real responses instead of just head nods. (3) Be silent while listening. When someone is asking a question—even a very long question—keep your mouth closed; don't interrupt. Keep your mind silent, too; don't respond until you've heard the whole question. (4) Use natural "minimal encouragers" such as nodding or tilting your head, smiling, widening your eyes, or even softly saying "uh huh."

- *Following skills:* Following skills ensure understanding between listener and questioner. (1) Make sure the audience understands the question by recapping it briefly in your own words if the questioner is hard to hear or by beginning your response in such a way that everyone in the audience knows what question you are answering. (2) Make sure you understand the question by paraphrasing it if it was asked in a confusing fashion or with an angry tone, or by asking the person to restate his question if it was unclear. When a question is unclear, use an *I* response rather than a *you* response, such as "*I'm* not sure *I* understand" rather than "*Your* question is confusing."

Dealing with difficult questions   Some questions are especially challenging because of their structure or word choice. Other questions cause problems because you don't know the answer. And finally, some questions are difficult because of the person who asked them.

- *Unclear questions:* These questions are confusing because of their structure, length, or word choice. (1) *Broad questions* about wide-ranging issues that could never be addressed in a limited time: either point out which part of the topic you'll discuss or offer to discuss the topic with the questioner at a later time. (2) *Vague questions* using terms like "this," "that notion," or "it": paraphrase the question in a way that defines your understanding of the term "this" or "it." (3) *Long multiquestions* stringing multiple questions together: either synthesize the many questions and offer a single response, start with the question you like best and avoid ones you don't want to address, or answer one part and then ask the questioner to remind you of the other questions— depending on the situation and the role of the questioner.

- *Questions framed in a limiting way:* Questioners knowingly or unknowingly sometimes frame questions in ways that can trap or at least restrict you. These questions need to be paraphrased to recast them for your own purpose. (1) *Forced-choice questions,* which use "either/or": remember that you can answer "both." (2) *Hypothetical questions* about future possibilities or the opinion of someone who is not in the room: either refuse to speculate or begin your response by noting that you are "not the CEO of Firestone," but from your vantage point, there are several issues to consider. (3) *Leading questions* that begin with a false premise, such as "When did you start manipulating the data?": recast the question: "If you are asking whether the data is accurate, yes, it is." (4) *Loaded questions* that use negative or emotionally charged language: don't repeat the negative words or get pulled into a question that you don't want to answer.

- *"Don't know" questions:* Sometimes, you absolutely don't know the answer. In such cases, say "I don't know." Even better, suggest where the person might find the answer. Better still, offer to get the answer yourself. For example, "Off the top of my head, I don't know the sales figures for that region, but I'll look them up and get them on your desk by tomorrow morning." Then be sure you follow up. Never hazard a guess unless you make it extremely clear that it is only a guess.

  In other cases, you may just need time to gather your thoughts. Here are a few stalling options: (1) *Repeat or paraphrase the question:* "You're wondering how to deal with the situation in the Ohio office"; (2) *Turn the question around:* "How do you think we should handle the situation in the Ohio office, Amy?"; (3) *Turn the question outward:* "What ideas do you all have about the Ohio situation?"; (4) *Reflect:* "Good question, Bill, let me think about it for a moment"; or (5) *Write:* If using a suitable visual aid, write down the main points of the question as you think.

Dealing with difficult questioners　Sometimes, questions may be difficult because of the person asking the question, rather than just the content itself. People may be difficult questioners because they are overly emotional, because of their tendency to pontificate, or because of their position (e.g., your boss or your client). Here are some tips for dealing with such questioners:

- *Be polite,* even to hostile questioners. Don't lower yourself to their level or snap at someone, saying "So, exactly what's your point? I didn't hear a question in there."

- *Lessen hostility* by pointing to common ground, in essence agreeing to disagree, for example, "We don't seem to agree on how to handle the customer service problem, but I hope we can at least agree that we both want to do what's best for most of our customers."

- *Paraphrase the feelings behind questions.* For example, you might paraphrase an emotional or sarcastic questioner by saying "You seem angry that you were not consulted about the new policy."

- *Interrupt repeat offenders.* If someone is a difficult questioner repeatedly, try a nonverbal interruption, such as putting up your hands, along with a verbal interruption such as "I'm sorry to interrupt, Lisa, but since time is limited, I want to make a brief comment about the important subject you've brought up, before we wrap up Q&A."

- *Look elsewhere afterwards.* After you answer a question, do not return your eye contact to the difficult questioner. If you look at a difficult audience member at the end of your response, you are just inviting him or her to ask yet another difficult question.

Delivering effective responses   Ideally, your responses will be easy to understand, interesting, and brief enough to maintain the interactive nature of a question-and-answer session.

- *Stick to your objective and your organization.* Answer the question, but always keep your presentation objective in mind. Even if you have lots of information for your answer, limit yourself to whatever advances your objective. Don't go off on rambling tangents. If necessary, divert the question back to your main ideas. If someone asks a question that you plan to cover later in your talk, try to answer it in a nutshell and then make it clear you'll cover the point in more detail later in your talk.

- *Provide a preview* if you have a long answer. For instance, you might say, "Yes, I do have several concerns about the new orientation program. Some of them deal with how the program is structured and others deal with logistical problems. In terms of structure . . ."

- *Make your responses interesting* by including brief examples or "sound bites"—colorful words or phrases that make your statements memorable. On the other hand, using abstract words or stringing several numbers together in a single sentence could make your response hard to follow. Find the balance between enough detail to be interesting and not so much that you ramble.

- *Keep the entire audience involved* in the Q&A session by calling on people from various locations in the room and by avoiding a one-to-one conversation with a single member of the audience. When you are responding, make eye contact with several people, not just the person who asked the question.

- *End with a summative statement.* If you opted to take questions at the end of your presentation, never let someone's tangential question close your presentation. Instead, end with a summative statement that synthesizes key messages from the Q&A session and connects them to your main message and your closing.

CHAPTER 5 OUTLINE

I. SELECT YOUR EQUIPMENT.
   1. Analyze your constraints and resources.
   2. Weigh the advantages and disadvantages.

II. COMPOSE YOUR MESSAGE TITLES.

III. CHOOSE YOUR CHART DESIGN.
   1. Data-driven charts to show "how much"
   2. Concept charts to show "how"
   3. Text visuals to show "what" or "why"

IV. ENSURE CONSISTENCY.
   1. Create a master template.
   2. Ensure structural and transitional consistency.
   3. Use parallelism for consistency.

V. STRIVE FOR SIMPLICITY AND READABILITY.
   1. Simplicity
   2. Readability
   3. Color issues

CHAPTER 5

Designing Your Visual Aids

The second implementation component is designing effective visual aids. Visual aids make your ideas clearer, more memorable, and more persuasive. The combination of seeing plus hearing is much more effective than either just seeing or just hearing. Furthermore, close to half of your audience is made up of "visual learners" who readily understand and recall visual images.

This chapter focuses on how to design visual aids by taking you through the process of creating them: (1) select your equipment, (2) compose your message titles, (3) choose your chart design, (4) ensure consistency, and (5) strive for simplicity and readability. Chapter 6 (pages 95–97) covers how to use your visual aids during your presentation.

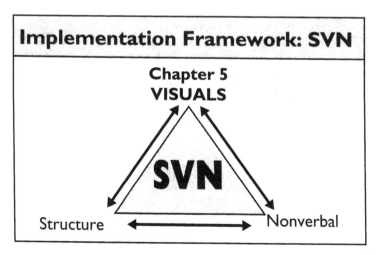

Implementation Framework: SVN

Chapter 5
VISUALS

SVN

Structure ⟷ Nonverbal

I. SELECT YOUR EQUIPMENT.

Before you begin to design your visuals, you need to know what equipment you will be using. Imagine, for example, how different your design would be for a computer projection or a flipchart or a handout. The following section offers ideas about analyzing your constraints and resources, then considers the advantages and disadvantages of each kind of equipment.

1. Analyze your constraints and resources.

Think through your constraints and resources then decide how to deal with them—as described below and summarized in the table on the facing page.

Audience/presenter constraints

- *Audience expectations:* Find out if your audience, organization, or culture expects you to use any certain kind of equipment—especially considering the presentation's level of formality and complexity.

- *Audience size:* The number of people in the audience determines how many handouts you'll need and influences what equipment you'll use.

- *Familiarity:* Only select options that you will be comfortable using.

Availability constraints   Don't make assumptions about availability of visual aid equipment. You need to know exactly what equipment is available, especially if you will be presenting in an unfamiliar location. Although you can bring equipment with you, toting a flipchart, overhead projector, or portable projection system may be either inconvenient or expensive or both.

- *High-tech options:* Before you decide to use the latest up-to-date high-tech equipment—such as Internet connections, computer, or video projection—find out what is available.

- *Low-tech options:* Similarly, don't assume that low-tech options such as flipcharts or white boards will automatically be there.

- *Room size:* Find out the dimensions of the room, what equipment and furniture (e.g., podium or screen) are built in and unmovable, and the distance between the projector and the screen. These issues will influence decisions such as font size.

* *Furniture:* Also check out furniture availability, such as permanent or movable chairs or tables. Remember, you will need tables if you want participants to write on your handouts, and you will need to arrange the furniture so everyone can see.

* *Lighting:* Finally, find out about the lighting, including window placement and dimming options. Whenever possible, try to present with the lights on.

RESOURCES AND OPTIONS	
Find out about ...	**Then, choose an option ...**
Audience size	• Small: Use flipbooks, laptop, board, or chart. • Large: Use flipbooks or projected visuals.
Audience expectations	• Go with the norm to "fit in." • Or, go against the norm to stand out.
Familiarity	• Use what's comfortable. • Learn new method; practice thoroughly. • Always familiarize yourself; see pages 95–97.
High-tech options	• Bring backup method in case of break down. • If necessary, bring laptop, adapters, etc.; learn password and operating systems.
Room and furniture	• Large: Avoid hand lettering; use large font. • Small: Don't crowd with too much equipment. • Chairs: Make sure everyone in every seat can see.
Lighting	• Choose options that work with lights on or slightly dimmed. • If you need the lights out, don't do so for too long.
Color capability and quality	• Arrive early and adjust color; desktop color ≠ screen color. • Know that it is hard to match printed color and projected color.

2. Weigh the advantages and disadvantages.

Visual aid equipment falls into four major categories, as described briefly below and summarized in the table on pages 58–59. In addition, see pages 95–97 for tips on how to use each of them.

Multimedia   Multimedia (or "high-tech") equipment projects images and sounds from a computer, the Internet, video, or audio sound systems.

- *Installed projectors:* Installed projectors are located permanently in one site. They may utilize CRT (cathode ray tube), LCD (liquid crystal display), or plasma technology. The individual quality of their resolution varies widely.

- *Portable projectors:* The quality of portable projectors varies also. For large groups, use LCD or DLP (digital light processing) technology large-screen options; for medium-sized groups, a large television monitor; and for small groups, a regular computer screen.

Still projection options   A second set of equipment involves "still" (or unanimated) projection.

- *Overhead projectors:* Overhead projectors are versatile: you can write on them as you speak and/or prepare them in advance. However, you need to use special acetate sheets and markers.

- *35-mm slide projectors:* Slides have the highest resolution, but if you want to change the slide order, you need to fast forward.

- *Document cameras:* With these projectors, you can project from copy on regular paper documents or objects. However, their resolution is not as high as overhead projectors.

Boards and flipcharts   Boards and flipcharts enhance group discussion and help create an informal environment.

- *Traditional boards* encourage discussion but do not provide hard copy.

- *Electronic copy boards* provide hard copy of what you write on the board.

- *"Live boards"* can be annotated from computers in multiple locations.

- *Flipchart* pages may be attached to the walls for further discussion.

Hard copy   Sometimes, it's important for the audience to have hard copy of some or all of what was discussed.

- *Specific handouts:* Some handouts provide detailed information to augment your visual aids in a specific section of your presentation, such as financial data or spreadsheets.

- *Flipbooks:* Another type of handout, called a "flipbook" (or "pitchbook" or "deck"), provides a hard copy of your presentation. Flipbooks can range from being professionally bound and printed in color to being simply stapled and printed in black and white. Sometimes flipbooks provide a copy of the projected visuals; other times, they are used alone, with the presenter talking about each page in turn. If you use a flipbook, always insert a page number on each page, so you can refer your audience to the right spot. Also, remember that wire-bound versions are easier to flip than those that are taped or stapled.

- *Slide copies:* Another option, less formal than a flipbook, is to provide copies of your slides, printed either two, three, or six per page.

VISUAL AID EQUIPMENT		
Equipment	**Main advantages**	**Main disadvantages**
Multimedia projection systems	*For all multimedia projections* Can use input from the web, PCs, video, etc.; can use animation; can use a variety of "build" techniques; can plug into audience's networked computers; can input numbers real time	May be complicated to use; usually need darkened room; not good for facilitating group discussion; cannot annotate real time; may appear too slick
Non-portable	*All of the above plus* CRT best resolution for full-screen; plasma saves installation space; both good for large groups	*All of the above plus* Not portable
Portable	LCD excellent resolution	Not easily portable
	Group data-display TV highest resolution	Can be seen by medium-sized groups only
	Regular computer screen avoids color distortion	Can be seen by small groups only
Video	Can use pause, fast forward, and rewind	May have format incompatibilities
Still projection systems	*For all still projection systems* Portability; less technically complex than multimedia; compatibility problems unlikely; easy to use	No animation; cannot use "build" techniques
Overhead projectors	*All of the above plus* Versatile: can write on them real time or prepare in advance; "random access"; easy to refer back to a previous slide; can adjust image size	*All of the above plus* Projector may block audience view; may be awkward to manipulate; may appear old-fashioned to some audiences

VISUAL AID EQUIPMENT		
Equipment	**Main advantages**	**Main disadvantages**
35-mm slide projectors	Highest resolution of all projection systems; projector does not block audience view, visible to large audiences	Darkened room; costly and time-consuming to produce; hard to refer back to a previous slide; cannot annotate real time
CCD document cameras	Projects image from any hard copy or 3D object	Less effective resolution than overheads or slides
	For all boards and charts	
Boards and charts	Brightly lit room; good for facilitating group discussion; can annotate real time	Inability to show complex images; usually too small to be seen by a large group
	All of the above plus	***All of the above plus***
Traditional black or white boards	Good for discussion; low-tech, unintimidating	Must erase to regain free space; no hard copy; may appear unprofessional
Electronic copy boards	Provides hard copy of what was on board; can be viewed on computer screens in multiple locations	Must erase to regain free space
"Live" boards	All of the above, plus can be annotated on-line in multiple locations	
Flipcharts	No electronics problems; may be attached to walls for further discussion	Large and clumsy to transport
Handouts		
Specific handouts	Provides hard copy; shows complex data; can be used for audience notetaking	Audience can read ahead and become distracted from what you are saying
Flipbooks	Good for audience "walk through"; good backup for computer slides; may be read by people who did not attend	Once printed, cannot change; cost of color printing

II. COMPOSE YOUR MESSAGE TITLES.

Once you've selected your equipment, but before you start to design, think about your important messages. Your key ideas and supporting points should determine what you choose to emphasize with your visual aids. Ideally, many of your ideas can actually be turned into titles and placed at the top of your visuals. If so, you will be using what are known as "message titles."

Focus on key ideas and supporting points.   Identify the meaningful messages in your presentation so you can decide which ones need to be seen as well as heard. Some messages tend to be important for every presentation; others relate to ideas that are specific to your talk.

- *Preview:* All presentations have a preview; therefore, this key idea is often turned into a visual aid. Your visual may be titled "preview," "agenda," "table of contents" or "overview," but no matter what you term it, it should reinforce the structure of your talk.

- *Recommendations/conclusions/objectives:* Depending upon whether you are selling or telling, one or more of these items may be a key idea that deserves to be seen as a visual aid.

- *Supporting messages:* You will also want visuals that support your recommendations and conclusions. Therefore, stand back from the potential encyclopedia of slides, sift through all the numbers and the information, and identify the most salient points. These are the messages you should highlight. They will influence what you include on your charts, and in many cases, they will become the titles of your visual aids.

Avoid "topic titles."   Most presenters, use what we call "topic titles." A topic title states the subject being discussed, but doesn't tell the viewer what message to take away.

For example, look at the following slide, with a topic title. The audience might see one or more of the following messages: "Sales are increasing," "Sales reached $90 million in 2000," or "Sales were $30 million in 1996." In this case, the viewer decides which message to see.

Example: ineffective topic title

As another example, notice how long it takes to make meaning out of the list below, which doesn't have a title.

1. Generating enthusiasm

2. Procrastinating

3. Missing the deadline

4. Blaming the innocent

5. Rewarding the nonparticipants

The missing title is "Five stages that doom a group project." As you can see, even when your visuals are made up of text only, message titles help viewers understand the main point by providing a context for the list.

Generally, use a topic title only when you have no message. For instance, if you want to lead a discussion about several trends, then you may want to put up a chart with a topic title and ask people to discuss what they see in the chart.

Use message titles.   Usually, however, you have a message you want to get across. So make it clear to your audience by using a "message title"—a short phrase or sentence with a point to it. For example, the following slide broadcasts the presenter's point with a message title.

Example: effective message title

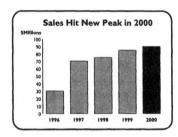

Clearly, message titles offer many important benefits, both to you and your audience.

- *Improve audience comprehension:* The audience will understand your visuals better because they see the main point easily.

- *Save processing time:* The audience can also process your visuals more quickly, thus speeding up the information–sharing process.

- *Increase your visuals' "stand-alone sense":* Message titles make "stand-alone sense," that is, they make sense on their own to someone seeing them for the first time. Stand-alone sense is important for audience members' comprehension—especially for latecomers, people who might tune out during part of your presentation, or for those who will see a copy of your slides or handouts later.

- *Help you with transitions:* Message titles also can make transitions easier for you, especially if they provide a link from one visual to the next. (See page 95 for more on how to state transitions.)

- *Improve flipbooks or handouts:* Message titles are especially helpful to make sure your audience grasps your main points if they are reading them—after the presentation or for the first time—in written form.

III. CHOOSE YOUR CHART DESIGN.

Choose your chart design only after you have created your message titles, so your messages will drive your selection. Visual expert Gene Zelazny lists seven types of designs, based on seven questions your charts might answer: (1) *What?* (text, pictures, video, or models), (2) *Where?* (maps, video, architectural plans), (3) *Who?* (organization charts, pictures, video), (4) *When?* (calendars, continuums, Gandt diagrams), (5) *How much?* (pie, bar, column charts, etc.), (6) *How?* (T-charts, matrix charts, Venn diagrams, etc.), and (7) *Why?* (text visuals or bullet lists). In most presentations, you'll want to use a combination of these charts to add variety to your visuals. Regardless of the design you choose, refer to the guidelines on pages 74–81 for tips on how to edit them.

In the following section, we concentrate on the three most prevalent kinds of charts:

1. *Data-driven charts* to show "how much" (such as pie and bar charts),
2. *Concept charts* to show "how" (such as matrix charts), and
3. *Text visuals* to show "what" or "why" (such as bullet lists).

1. Data-driven charts to show "how much"

Quantitative information is easier for your audience to comprehend if you show it on data-driven charts rather than in a data dump of numbers. Don't project a table of numbers; instead, find the message you wish to convey that is supported by those numbers.

Once you have identified your message, consider it carefully and determine what type of comparison it seems to be making. Does it discuss how one part relates to the whole (pie chart)? Or does it comment on how something is changing over time (line or column charts)? The table on page 64 offers greater detail about how to match your message to a chart.

Before you actually create your chart, be sure to review the labeling alternatives on page 65, experiment with the emphasis techniques on page 66, and read the guidelines on pages 74–81.

EXAMPLES OF DATA-DRIVEN CHARTS

To show ...	Use a chart like this ...
Components of one item • Percentages • Shares • Proportions	Pie Exploded Pie
Comparison of multiple items • Rank • More or less than • Difference among	Bar Column
Components of multiple items • Percentages • Shares • Proportions	Subdivided Bar Subdivided Column
Changes over time or frequency • Increase/decrease • Fluctuations • Trends	Line Column
Correlation • Relation • Pattern • Deviation from pattern	Scatter Paired Bar Item

LABELING CHARTS

1. Preferred option:
Label inside section

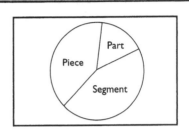

2. Second best option:
Label just outside section

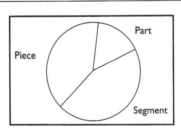

3. Third best option:
Label and connect to section with line

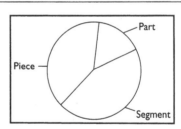

4. Worst option:
Use a legend

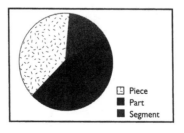

SHOWING EMPHASIS ON CHARTS

1. Contrasting color

Company B ranks second.

Company A
Company B
Company C
Company D

2. Lines

Product C uses far less graphite than other products.

Pathite
Graphite
Snafite

A　B　C　D　E

3. Arrows

Sales declined dramatically in March.

Jan　Feb　Mar　Apr　May

4. "Exploded" off

East generates the smallest share of profits.

East
North
South
West

2. Concept charts to show "how"

Just as data-driven charts help your audience process quantitative data better than a "data dump" of numbers, concept charts help your audience recall qualitative concepts better than a "word dump" of endless bullet lists. Concept charts add excitement to your visuals, prevent you from overusing text visuals, and especially appeal to the visual learners in your audience. For example, compare the following two agenda charts:

Agenda example: words only

Adopt a strategic approach

1. Analyze the audience.
2. Identify your intent.
3. Make your message memorable.

Same agenda: using concept chart

Adopt a strategic approach

2. intent

AIM

1. audience   3. message

The table on the next page provides some ideas for concept charts. For many more examples, refer to the Howell book listed in the bibliography.

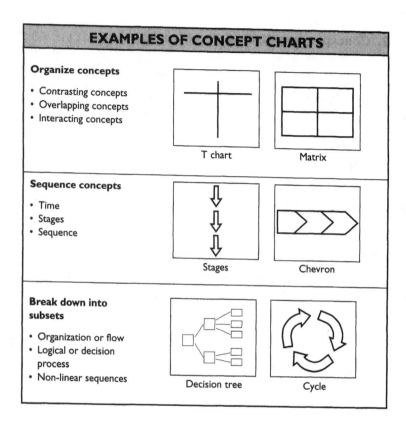

EXAMPLES OF CONCEPT CHARTS

Organize concepts

• Contrasting concepts
• Overlapping concepts
• Interacting concepts

T chart   Matrix

Sequence concepts

• Time
• Stages
• Sequence

Stages   Chevron

Break down into subsets

• Organization or flow
• Logical or decision process
• Non-linear sequences

Decision tree   Cycle

2. Text visuals to show "what" or "why"

Although text visuals are not visual by definition, there are still some visual issues to consider when designing them.

Avoid centering.   A common misunderstanding about visual design is that titles or text should be centered. In reality, centering lines of text can make them harder to read. In most cases, use left justification for both titles and text.

Centering text doesn't improve readability.

The lines may look balanced.

Left-justification is still easier to read.

Centering long message titles looks odd, especially

when they wrap to the next line.

Use indentation effectively.   Also be sure to use effective indentation as a design element in text visuals, as shown in the following examples:

Ineffective indentation

• Here is an example of an ineffective bullet indentation in which the bullet does not stand out very much because the subsequent lines "wrap around" it.

  • Here is another example of an ineffective bullet indentation in which the bullet does not stand out very much either—this time because only the first line is indented.

Effective indentation

   • Here is an example of an effective bullet indentation. All of the lines in the section are indented equally, so the bullet "stands out" on its own. For effective bullets, use the "hanging indent" feature in your software program.

IV. ENSURE CONSISTENCY.

As a group, all of your visuals need to look consistent and coherent—not like a mishmash of unrelated items. This section covers consistency of template, presentation structure, and grammatical structure (parallelism).

I. Create a master template.

One of the best ways to ensure consistency is to create a master template. Avoid the prepared templates available in software packages; most of them are cluttered and unsuitable for professional presentations; the few that are suitable may be overused and therefore boring.

- *Design a single pattern,* including layout, titles and subtitles, fonts, point size, bullet points, graphics, and use of color (as described on pages 80–81). Stick with this pattern except for extreme emphasis.

- *Choose a consistent "build" device.* Figure out how you are going to disclose information within each slide. Choose a uniform and simple "animation" function, such as "build and dim" or "no animation." Avoid distracting effects—such as dissolving, spiraling, or flying bullets—which draw more attention to themselves than they do to the message.

- *Consider team consistency.* Consistency is especially important in team presentations. Create one master template for everyone in the team to use. Otherwise, the presentation will look like a series of individual presentations thrown together at the last minute.

- *Select a consistent page set up.* Use a horizontal page setup ("landscape") for slides, overheads, and decks. Use a consistent page setup—either "landscape" or "portrait"—for handouts.

- *Follow corporate identity standards.* Follow any guidelines your company may have about how to incorporate its logo or colors into presentation materials. Companies, just like individual presenters, benefit from using consistent visual communication.

2. Ensure structural and transitional consistency.

Use your visuals to reinforce and clarify the structure of your presentation.

Preview and support slides

- *Show a preview* or agenda visual early in the presentation; insert a table of contents showing page numbers in the beginning of a deck.
- *Use the same wording* that appears on your preview (or the table of contents) consistently in the message titles of your other visuals throughout the presentation. For example, if you say "Financial projection" in the table of contents, don't say "Spreadsheet analysis" in the title of your supporting visual.

Transition devices

- *Option 1: Repeated preview slide:* In longer presentations, one way to emphasize structure and ensure consistency is to return to the preview slide—with the next section highlighted—each time you move to a new major section in your presentation. The examples below show two different ways to highlight a repeated preview slide.

Using box to show transition

Analyze the audience

- Who are they?
- What do they know?
- What do they feel?

Using "dim" to show transition

Analyze the audience

- Who are they?
- **What do they know?**
- What do they feel?

- *Option 2: Trackers:* Another way to reinforce the structure of a long presentation visually is to use "trackers"—words or symbols that identify the section of the presentation currently under discussion. They often appear in the corners of a slide or on a presentation deck. Trackers need to be visible, but avoid making them so large that they compete with other text. Two samples of trackers appear below.

Tracker: lower right corner

Analyze your audience

- Who are they?
- What do they know?
- What do they feel?

Strategy:
AIM

Tracker: upper left corner

Strategy:
AIM

Analyze your audience

- Who are they?
- What do they know?
- What do they feel?

3. Use parallelism for consistency.

Using parallel structure makes it easier for your audience to follow your points and easier for you to state them. Be aware of two kinds of parallelism.

Use grammatical parallelism. Use grammatical parallelism on text charts—that is, make sure the first word in a series is consistent with the other first words in that series.

Ineffective grammatical parallelism

1. Overall issues and their effect
2. Templates guarantee stylistic patterns
3. Use parallel structure on individual slides

Effective grammatical parallelism

1. Consider overall consistency
2. Create a master template
3. Use parallel structure

Use conceptual parallelism. Text charts need to be not only grammatically parallel, they also need what communication expert JoAnne Yates dubs "conceptual parallelism"—that is, ideas of equal importance should be shown at equal hierarchical level. In the following example, "analyze the audience" is the major point, with the other items being subpoints, since they each offer information about how to perform the analysis.

Ineffective conceptual parallelism

- Analyze the audience
- Use the three questions
- Examine your assumptions

Effective conceptual parallelism

Analyze the audience

- Use the three questions
- Examine your assumptions

V. STRIVE FOR SIMPLICITY AND READABILITY.

The most important design guideline is very basic: keep your visuals simple. This advice applies to your overall design and to each individual visual.

I. Simplicity

Overall simplicity

- *Don't create too many visual aids.* In general, do not show many more than one visual per minute, and use far fewer if your slides are complex. However, don't overload each individual visual in a misguided effort to use fewer total visuals.

- *Don't overload your visuals.* Visuals, especially projected visuals, must be easy to comprehend quickly. Author David Peoples compares visuals to billboards, pointing out that the audience needs to take in the message with a glance. Flipbooks, especially if designed to be take-away reports, can accommodate more information per page; however, if a flipbook is your primary visual aid medium, then it also needs to contain a lot of white space and limited information on each page.

- *Don't bombard the audience with auditory, visual, or animated clutter.* This clutter includes such things as startling sounds, silly clip art, excessive color, or animation effects that cause all your bullet points to fly up, down, and across the screen. This advice applies especially to software program default options that result in clutter.

- *Plan to get rid of already used visuals* so they don't compete with new visuals—or with you, the presenter—for the audience's attention.

- *Don't overdo visuals on multiple equipment.* If you are using more than one type of visual aid equipment (e.g., slides plus a video clip plus a flipchart to record audience reactions), don't overdo it. Simply switching back and forth from one type of equipment to another takes time.

Simplicity in your data-driven charts

- *Eliminate "chartjunk."* The first slide on the facing page is anything but simple. It is overloaded with what design expert Edward Tufte terms "chartjunk." Chartjunk includes all those distractions—such as three-dimensional figures, grid lines, legends, and crosshatching—which confuse the viewer. The second slide shown at right shows the same information, this time presented without chartjunk.

- *Override computer-default chartjunk.* Chartjunk temptations are built into presentation software packages. Therefore, before you begin designing charts, regain control of your computer. (1) *Change the default settings* to eliminate grid lines, tick marks, crosshatching, and legends. (2) *Choose two-dimensional figures* instead of 3D views. (3) *Modify chart elements.* Make narrow bars and columns wider while decreasing the space between them; eliminate the overuse of exploding pie pieces, and increase the boldness of trend lines so they are actually visible on line charts. (4) *Insert labels manually.* Since software packages do not clearly label bars, pie slices, or lines, plan to type and insert labels manually. (5) *Modify automatic color choices* to eliminate the overuse of color and ensure the visibility of important information.

- *Keep data points to a minimum.* A chart will be confusing if it uses too many data points, such as (1) *Pie slices:* Usually, more than six pie slices are too complex to label and project. Consider using an "other" slice to streamline the chart. (2) *Columns:* Once you have six columns on your column chart, consider using a line chart instead. (3) *Lines:* In a line chart, more than three lines make the trends hard to differentiate.

Ineffective chart: chartjunk

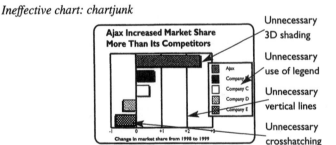

Effective chart: no chartjunk

Simplicity in your concept charts   Concept charts (as explained on pages 67–68) can effectively show "how"—or they can be so overloaded with arrows, lines, boxes, and description that they merely baffle the audience. If you need to show a complex diagram, "build" it and discuss it in stages, perhaps using color to highlight the section you are discussing and adding arrows one at a time. The two slides below show an overly complex and a simplified version of the same diagram.

Ineffective chart: overloaded

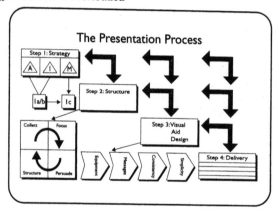

Effective chart: simplified

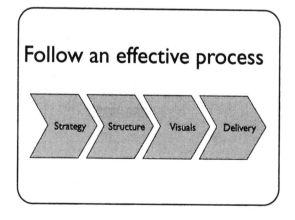

Simplicity in your text visuals   Keeping it simple applies to visuals with words as well as to those with images. Just because you *can* fit everything on one chart doesn't mean you *should*. For instance, the chart below doesn't look inviting and certainly wouldn't sound interesting if you read it to your audience word for word.

- *Use the "six-by-six" guideline.* As a general guideline, think "six by six"—a maximum of six lines per visual and an average of six words per line. Longer text visuals can turn a presentation into a group reading session.

- *Keep the lines short.* If you have more than one line that needs to be wrapped, either simplify the line into partial phrases instead of complete sentences or break the line into a main point with subpoints.

- *Break the six-by-six guideline if necessary.* If absolutely necessary to break the guideline, consider building the lines one at a time or chunking the information into two or three parts. Do not, however, violate the "six-by-six" guideline on slide after slide after slide.

Ineffective chart: too wordy

Text Visuals Can Hold a Great Deal of Information

- You can put lots of print on a horizontal
  chart, without wrapping text lines too many times.
- Even if you had 12 bullet points, you *could* fit
  them all on a single slide.
- You might even decide to change the line spacing
  to squeeze in your last idea.
- Your font size might still be readable in the back
  row. But, nevertheless, the slide still has way too
  many words on it.
- Writing complete sentences means you can
  read this wonderful prose to your audience.
- If you make margins really wide and use the
  space under the bullets, you can squeeze more in,
  too.

2. Readability

One of the most common problems with visuals is that they can't be read—for reasons ranging from size to layout to color combinations. The following guidelines will help you avoid these readability problems.

Choose a readable font.   Computers offer a wide array of fonts. Serif fonts have extenders at the ends of each letter, such as the font you are reading now. Sans serif fonts do not have such extenders.

Examples of serif fonts

Times New Roman, Bookman, Century Schoolbook

Examples of sans serif fonts

Arial, Helvetica, Comic Sans

Generally, choose a serif font for a more traditional look and for densely-printed documents. Use sans serif fonts for a more modern look and for items to be read on a small screen (because screens have lower display capabilities than paper).

Use readable letter size   The minimum size you can use depends on your choice of equipment, as explained below. In addition, it depends on the font itself. For example, Times New Roman is much smaller than Verdana.

- *For projection:* As you select font sizes for projected visuals, generally, use font sizes over 18 point. The only exception would be for secondary items (such as an axis label or a source), but if you plan to use such small fonts, be sure to test them. In addition, be sure the size differentiation between your titles and the text clearly distinguishes one from the other. Titles should be 32 point or larger; text should be about 24 point.

- *For flipbooks and handouts:* When creating flipbooks or other types of handouts, text should be at least 11- or 12-point. In handouts, you can differentiate between the headings and text by using graphic variations such as bold titles and regular text.

- *For handwritten lettering:* As a general guide for hand lettering, try to keep your letters at least two inches high for every thirty feet of viewing distance. If your handwriting is hard to read or the marker has a fine point, then use even larger lettering to ensure readability.

Avoid letterjunk   Your computer tempts you with all sorts of ways to highlight text. Wise options for highlighting include plain text, boldface, or italics. Be careful when using italics, however; in some fonts, they are hard to read on slides. Be wary of using options such as underlining, shadow lettering, outlining, and embossing because they impair readability.

shadow lettering, outlining, and **embossing**

Especially avoid using combinations of options, which result in:

<u>**overwhelming letterjunk.**</u>

Avoid all capital letters   Some people think that putting a line of text in all capital letters makes that text stand out:

WHILE A LINE OF ALL CAPITAL LETTERS MAY APPEAR LARGER THAN REGULAR TEXT, USING ALL CAPITAL LETTERS ACTUALLY HURTS READABILITY; THEREFORE, USE ALL CAPITAL LETTERS SPARINGLY.

Look at the same sentence again, this time without all capital letters:

While a line of all capital letters may appear larger than regular text, using all capital letters hurts readability. Therefore, use all capital letters SPARINGLY.

Therefore, never use all capital letters for long lines of text. Instead, use "sentence case" for your visuals—that is, capitalize the first word in a line, not every word in a title, or every letter in a line.

3. Color issues

Color is another visual element that is available, in some form, with most visual aid options—ranging from computer-generated visuals shown on screen or printed in a flipbook, to multicolored markers for flipcharts or whiteboards, to video clips. When used skillfully and with some restraint, color can be a powerful design tool.

Keep your color palette simple.

- *Don't overdo it.* You can create hundreds of colors with your computer; just be sure you don't. Do not weaken the power of color by overusing it; use it to enhance your message and to communicate.

- *Avoid the "fruit salad effect."* Design expert Jan White refers to the overuse of color as the "fruit salad effect." White even goes so far as to recommend using only two colors in addition to black, because "the more colors there are, the more difficult it is to remember the meaning each carries."

- *Consider your audience and resources.* Some audiences expect color visuals; for others, color visuals may seem too slick and counter to cultural norms. In addition, color printing is expensive for flipbooks or overhead slides.

Use color for a reason.

- *Use color to highlight and reinforce your structure.* Viewers sense color relationships clearly and quickly—so they will stay better attuned to your structure if you use color to emphasize it.

- *Use a consistent pattern.* Throughout the presentation, use the same color choices for background, titles, text, bullets, trackers, and so forth. Alter this pattern only when you want to make one slide stand out from the others.

- *Use color for emphasis.* Viewers will look at anything that is not black and white first, so use color to highlight what you want them to look at.

If your message is . . .	Use bright color for . . .	Use muted color for . . .	Override software default that . . .
Emphasizing a certain "slice of the pie"	For that particular slice only	All the other slices	Automatically colors each slice a different color

Choose visible background/text color combinations.

- *Use deep contrast.* The best combinations for background and text colors are those that offer great contrast. For example, on a clear background or white page, use black or deep blue text to offer such contrast. On a blue background, choose white and yellow for highly contrasting text colors.

- *Avoid bad combinations.* Some color combinations just don't work. For example, bright red lettering on a bright blue background is very hard to see.

- *Consider your medium.* Certain background colors work better for certain media. (1) *Flipbooks:* White or pale colors usually are better than dark backgrounds for flipbooks; dark blocks of color frequently look "streaky" when printed and take longer to print. (2) *Slides:* Overheads often look better with clear or pale backgrounds, but 35-mm slides look best with dark backgrounds. (3) *Computer slide shows:* When designing computer-generated slide shows, blue backgrounds and clear backgrounds tend to be the safest options. The better choice is the one that looks good and enables you to keep the lights on.

- *Consider printing issues.* If you print color visuals in black and white, new visibility issues surface. For example, pie slices that are red and blue may print as the same shade of gray.

- *Test your colors.* For computer projection, always test your colors on the screen, because different projection equipment and room lighting will affect results. For printed materials, beware of differences among different printing equipment.

Think about audience interpretations.   People do not view and interpret color the same way. All audience members will have certain associations with color.

- *Cultural associations:* Color associations vary by culture. For example, different colors may be associated with death and funerals: black in the Anglo-American culture, white in some Eastern cultures, and yellow in some Moslem cultures. Often, the colors of a country's flag have a special meaning in that country.

- *Business associations:* Be aware of business associations such as "in the red" or the color green being linked to money in the United States.

- *Company associations:* Color may also have organizational associations. For example, if your company's logo is dark blue, then you might use this color on a bar chart to distinguish your company from the competition.

CHAPTER 6 OUTLINE

I. ANALYZE YOUR NONVERBAL SKILLS.
   1. Body stance and movement
   2. Hand and arm gestures
   3. Eye contact and facial expression
   4. Vocal traits
   5. Space and objects around you

II. ENHANCE YOUR NONVERBAL DELIVERY.
   1. Practice your content and timing.
   2. Practice with your visual aids.
   3. Prepare for your specific equipment.

III. MANAGE YOUR NERVOUS SYMPTOMS.
   1. General techniques
   2. Physical techniques
   3. Mental techniques
   4. Last-minute techniques

CHAPTER 6

Refining Your Nonverbal Delivery

The third component of presentation implementation consists of your nonverbal delivery skills—how you look and sound to your audience. We all know that nonverbal delivery is crucial to a presentation's success. Even so, "perfect" delivery is not necessary, and, in fact, may not even be possible, since different people prefer different delivery styles. Therefore, when working on your delivery, don't try for perfection. Instead, use the suggestions offered in this chapter to (1) analyze your nonverbal delivery skills, (2) enhance your nonverbal delivery, and (3) manage your nervous symptoms.

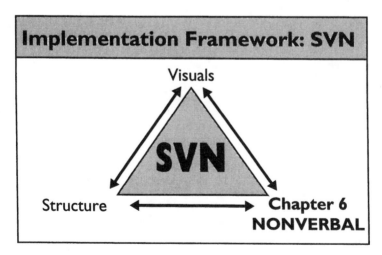

I. ANALYZE YOUR NONVERBAL SKILLS.

Many nonverbal elements affect your delivery. Some are your own behaviors, such as your hand and foot placement. You can observe these by watching yourself on videotape or by rehearsing in front of a mirror. Other elements are separate from you, such as your use of visual aids and the space around you. You can improve these by rehearsing in the place where you will be presenting. All of them, however, are situational—varying by personality, room size, and culture.

1. Body stance and movement

One important way you communicate nonverbally is through your full-body stance and movement.

Distracting positions   As you have no doubt witnessed, some speakers position and move their bodies in ways that are distracting.

- *The "hip sit":* Some presenters put all their weight on one leg, resting in a position called the "hip sit" or "parking on your hip." This stance can cause them to shift back and forth or from one side to the other.
- *Odd feet positions:* A stance with feet too far apart looks like a "human easel" or a "cowpoke straddle," with feet too close together like "the toppling tower," with toes pointed out like "the duck."
- *Moving positions:* Presenters often rock, sway, or bounce in one place, constantly pace, or move nonstop—all of which are noticeable and distracting.
- *Leaning positions:* Leaning stances known as the "podium clutch" or "table lean," leave the presenter's legs free to swing, wrap, tap, twist, and distract throughout the presentation.
- *Seated positions:* When seated, some presenters swivel, lean, or slouch in their chairs.

Effective informal positions   In informal situations, sitting down may be just fine as long as you aren't doing anything extreme or distracting. Less formal standing postures may be fine, also; but, if you're leaning against a table, make sure you don't swing your legs or move your feet.

Effective formal positions   In formal situations, you have fewer options.

• *Formal "opening stance":* To create a formal opening stance: (1) Place your feet shoulder-width apart, rather than very close together or extremely far apart. (2) Distribute your weight evenly, using both legs equally for support. (3) Divide your weight between your heels and the balls of your feet, rather than leaning back on your heels or up on your toes. (4) Position your feet straight out, avoiding a "duck" stance by making sure your toes are not farther apart than your heels. (5) Avoid locking your knees.

• *Formal movement:* In formal situations, it's fine to move for a reason— to emphasize a key point on your visual aid, for example, or to move closer to the audience to signal that you are seeking questions.

Positions in different environments   Room size may affect your movement; for example, small rooms usually don't allow for as much movement as larger rooms. Seating arrangements may also be a factor; for example, in a "U-shape" arrangement, don't move too far into the center of the room, since the people on the side will only have a view of your back.

2. Hand and arm gestures

Many presenters report that their hands and arms feel very awkward when they present. They don't know where to put their hands or their arms feel too long. Therefore, consider these tips:

Discover your natural gesturing style.   To do so, try to get a sense of your natural gestures in relaxed situations such as at a party, and/or when you are seated. Get feedback either from people who know you well or from watching yourself on videotape. The feedback should give you information about your natural style, such as how much you gesture, how dramatically, and with what nervous habits.

Avoid distracting gestures.   Once you learn about your natural gesturing habits, you will want to work on eliminating distracting gestures and avoid overusing favorites. Many of the following hand and arm positions have descriptive or humorous names; none of them send the right nonverbal message to the audience.

- *The gun-shot victim* clings to his upper arm with one hand.
- *The commander* places both hands on her hips.
- *The armless presenter* leaves his hands behind his back.
- *The chilly presenter* crosses her arms over her chest.
- *The pocket jingler* places his hands in his pockets, shaking his keys or coins.
- *The exposed presenter* clasps her hands in front of her, where a "figleaf" would be.
- *The clutcher* grasps a pen, pointer, or anything else he can find, instead of putting the object down.
- *The slapper* slaps her palms against her thighs.

Gesture naturally, as you would in conversation.   Aside from avoiding distracting gestures, you want your gesturing style as a speaker to match the style you use in conversations.

- *Refine; don't obsess.* Remember that you don't need to be perfect. You might slap your thigh, overuse your favorite gesture, and still accomplish your presentation objective. Therefore, work to refine your gesturing style, but don't obsess about it.

- *Avoid extremes.* Most of your gestures should be below your face and above your waist. Watch out for extremes: if you keep your hands at your sides and use only tiny flapping gestures, you might look meek; on the other hand, if you use lots of huge gestures down to your knees and then up over your head, you may look more like a cheerleader than a business presenter.

- *Use pointing carefully.* Reserve pointing for visual aids, not for people. Or try "friendly pointing" with your whole hand, keeping your palms sideways.

Consider the environment. To a certain extent, of course, the appropriate size of gestures depends on the environment.

- *Think about the size of the room.* In a large room, gestures can be rather large and still look appropriate; however, speaking in a small space or on a TV screen requires smaller gestures.

- *Think about your audience.* Some people like presenters who gesture often. Others prefer limited gesturing.

- *Think about the culture.* Remember that some cultures generally use more expansive gestures, others are more restrained. Also, find out about vulgar or insulting gestures in different cultures.

3. Eye contact and facial expression

Your face plays a crucial role in your nonverbal delivery style: your eye contact connects you with your audience, and your face communicates your interest, enthusiasm, and confidence.

Eye contact   Most U.S. business audiences want you to "look them in the eye"—a mark of honesty and confidence according to cultural norms. Here are some tips to assist you as you use eye contact to connect to your audience:

- *Find a friendly face.* If you are nervous, making eye contact with a supportive audience member might actually calm you down. The smiles and nods you see from the friendly face can help you get through difficult parts of your presentation and boost your energy level.

- *Have "little conversations."* Imagine you are speaking to one person at a time to decrease your intimidation and to develop a more natural delivery style.

- *Look long enough to complete a thought.* You don't want to stare or to seem robotic and darting. Therefore, look at a person's whole face long enough to complete your thought and register a reaction.

- *Locate key decision makers.* When delivering a persuasive presentation, be sure to check the reactions of any key decision makers, without focusing on them exclusively.

- *Use your body to make eye contact,* not just your head. In a wide room, if you simply move your head from one side to the other, the audience may begin to feel as if they are watching you watch a tennis match.

- *Adjust for large audiences.* If you are speaking before a crowd of hundreds, try to find a person in each section of the audience to use as an anchor point for your eye contact. If you start looking at the people sitting all around these anchors, then you'll be sure you are not ignoring one section of the audience. When lighting prevents you from seeing anyone in the audience, you'll still need to give the appearance of making eye contact to all parts of the room.

Facial expression   Avoid the stony, deadpan expression of ineffective and nervous speakers. Instead, relax your face and use natural facial expressions.

- *Use conversational facial expression.* Like gesturing, facial expression patterns are very speaker specific. Regardless of your natural style, use facial expression, like eye contact, to connect with your audience.

- *Smile when appropriate.* Conversational facial expression does not mean you have to smile all the time. For example, you might want to smile when you introduce yourself, but avoid smiling out of nervousness or when discussing serious or sad topics.

- *Interact with the audience.* Try the technique of looking at someone in the audience with "appropriate" facial expression and mirroring that person's expression. For example, if you want to remember to smile, look at a friendly face whose smile might help you express one of your own.

4. Vocal traits

Ideally, your voice should sound natural and interesting. The easiest way to achieve this is to avoid reading or memorizing (as described on page 93). If you attempt to read to your audience, you'll have a much harder time sounding natural. Reading causes most people to stumble over words or phrases and to use unnatural vocal patterns. Memorizing also leads to an artificial vocal style. As speakers try to recall words, they often sound rehearsed.

Vocal "image" is a combination of several factors: volume, rate, inflection, and enunciation.

Volume (loud or soft)   You need to be loud enough for everyone in your audience to hear you.

- *Speak to the back row.* If you naturally have a soft, hard-to-hear voice, begin by speaking to the person farthest away from you and try not to let your volume drop. Most likely, you sound much louder to yourself than you do to the audience.

- *Add volume without adding vocal strain.* If you need to increase volume, learn how to add volume without creating vocal strain. Begin by imagining that you are perched on a balcony, with the audience sitting below you. When you attempt to "send your voice" down to the audience, you will produce sound by pushing from your diaphragm rather than your throat. Your volume will increase, but you won't sound as if you are shouting and you won't strain your vocal cords.

- *Watch for "volume drops."* Volume sometimes drops to inaudible levels in two situations. (1) *At the end of sentences:* If you notice your voice trailing off at the end of sentences, try pausing at the end of each sentence, then taking in enough air to keep your volume up all the way through the end of the next sentence. (2) *As you introduce your visuals:* If your volume drops when you turn to introduce your visual aids, either try talking to people in the back row or stop talking if you need to turn away to put up a new visual.

- *Avoid an overwhelming volume.* If you naturally have a loud, booming voice, you also need to do a "sound check." Ask someone to stand in the back of the room and tell you if you are overwhelming them with sound.

- *Vary your volume.* Try to vary volume to add interest. If you say some words or phrases loudly, you will be able to add emphasis. Sometimes dropping your volume in an unexpected way may also grab attention.

Rate (fast or slow)

- *Avoid talking too fast.* When some speakers feel anxious or excited, they speak faster than usual. If you are a fast talker, you'll need to slow your pace when presenting. Practice speaking at a much slower rate than you would usually use, even though it will sound very unnatural and feel artificial to you.

- *Avoid talking too slowly.* If you naturally speak at a slow rate, try speeding up, at least when the material is simple or else try focusing on other vocal elements to add variety to your style.

- *Add pauses to alter your rate.* One of the best ways to alter rate is to add pauses. Pause for commas, periods, and after a key message. Take a deep breath before you continue.

- *Keep in mind your culture or accent.* (1) Vary your rate to be understood in the culture or region where you are speaking. Northeasterners, for example, tend to speak quickly and Southerners more slowly. (2) If you have an accent that the audience is not used to hearing, be sure you speak slowly, especially when you introduce yourself. (3) Similarly, if some of your audience members are non-native speakers, try to speak a bit more slowly than usual so these people can get used to your voice.

Inflection (high or low)   The term "inflection" refers to variation in pitch. Generally, women have higher-pitched voices and men have lower-pitched voices.

- *Use effective inflection.* Using varied inflection creates lively and energetic delivery. Maintaining the same pitch throughout your presentation sounds robotic and boring.

- *Avoid a high-pitched voice.* A high-pitched voice can decrease your credibility. Therefore, if you have a high-pitched voice, try to drive it downward to sound stronger and more authoritative.
- *Avoid monotonous pitch.* On the other hand, if you have a very deep voice, you need to avoid a monotonous sound.

Enunciation (articulation) "Enunciation" refers to how clearly you pronounce your words.

- *Using formal enunciation:* In formal situations, formal enunciation can be important. Take the time to say each syllable of a word. Instead of saying "gunna," say "going to."
- *Using informal enunciation:* In informal situations, using such careful enunciation may sound stiff. In these cases, you can add contractions and use other informal elements to make yourself sound less formal.
- *Avoiding troublesome words:* Some people find that pronouncing certain words—such as "similarly"—gives them trouble. Either avoid using such words or else breathe before you say them.

Filler words (verbal pauses) Filler words are short sounds that take the place of pauses—such as *uh, er, um,* and *you know.* Using a few *ah*s or *um*s is natural for many speakers; if used occasionally, they are not a problem.

- *Avoid overused fillers.* If you overuse fillers, try to add pauses, become comfortable with silence, and improve your breathing patterns.
- *Avoid conjunctions as filler words.* Some speakers have developed what communication expert Joann Baney calls "advanced filler words." These speakers create amazingly long, compound, complex sentences using conjunctions such as *and* or *so.*

5. Space and objects around you

Another component of nonverbal communication is based on how you handle the space and objects around you.

Space   Think about your choices for dealing with seating, height, and distance.

- *Choices for seating:* The way you arrange the chairs for a presentation will communicate nonverbally the kind of interaction you want to have with your audience. Choose straight lines of chairs for the least interactive sessions. Choose U-shaped lines of chairs to encourage more interaction. When presenting at a table, remember that round tables are friendlier and less formal than rectangular ones.

- *Choices for height and distance:* The higher you are in relation to your audience, the more formal the atmosphere you are establishing nonverbally. Therefore, the most formal presentations might be delivered from a stage or a platform. In a semiformal situation, you might stand while your audience sits. To make the situation even less formal, place yourself and your audience at the same level; sit together at a round table or seat yourself in front of the group. Similarly, the closer you are to your audience, the less formal you appear.

Objects around you   Another aspect of environmental nonverbal communication has to do with the objects you choose to have around you and those you opt to wear.

- *Objects between you and the audience:* In general, the more objects you place between yourself and the audience, the more formal the interaction. To increase formality, keep a podium, desk, or table between yourself and the audience. To decrease formality, stand or sit without any objects or furniture separating you from your audience.

- *Dress:* Think about audience expectations and your comfort as you select your wardrobe. Dress to project the image that you want to create. In addition, dress appropriately for the audience, the occasion, the organization, and the culture. For instance, what is appropriate in the fashion industry may not be totally appropriate in the banking industry, and what is appropriate in a company with a business casual dress code may be out of place in a company requiring formal attire. Avoid distracting apparel or accessories such as jewelry that makes noise when you gesture or ties that become the focus of attention.

II. ENHANCE YOUR NONVERBAL DELIVERY.

Once you have analyzed your nonverbal skills, you can enhance them by using the techniques covered in the following section.

I. Practice your content and timing.

One of the things presenters worry about is how to remember what to say. Some presenters write out a word-for-word manuscript—which leads to decreased audience interaction and artificial-sounding delivery. Others try to memorize their presentations—which is unrealistic, given business time constraints. Yet others read from their visuals—which leads them to maintain eye contact only with the screen and to overload their visuals with too many words.

Speak from an outline.   Instead, we recommend speaking from notes in outline form. By doing so, you will avoid having to memorize or read from a manuscript or your visuals—yet you will have the confidence of knowing your main ideas are close at hand should you need them. You can create your outline notes either before or after you design your visuals, using these guidelines:

- *Use phrases only.* Do not write complete sentences; instead, print very short phrases for each point and subpoint.
- *Use large lettering.* Use lettering large enough so that you can see it at arm's length. Leave lots of white space.
- *Add reminders.* You can also add reminders to yourself, such as "speak slowly" or "show line chart now."

Use notecards or paper.   Think about whether to write your outline on paper or notecards.

- *Paper:* Some presenters put their outline on 8½-by-11 inch paper. The disadvantage of paper is that it is awkward to hold or carry; you will need to put your notes down on a table, desk, or lectern when you are not using them.
- *Notecards:* Most experts suggest writing your outline on 5-by-7 or 4-by-6 inch cards, either handwritten or printed from a computer using a large font. Notecards have many advantages: they are easier to hold and carry if you want to move around as you present; they allow you

to add to, subtract from, or rearrange your materials easily; and their limited size reminds you to avoid writing notes that are full sentences. Typically, one notecard should hold about five minutes' worth of presentation reminders.

* *Visual aid printouts:* Other presenters print their slides two per page and then add their speaking notes. If you use this technique, cut the pages into half sheets to avoid holding the floppy and unprofessional-looking large sheets.

Rehearse.   Once you have your notes in hand, it's time to rehearse your presentation.

* *Practice out loud, on your feet.* Knowing your content and saying it aloud are two completely different activities, so do not practice by sitting and reading over your notecards. Instead, practice out loud and on your feet. For an important presentation, rehearse the entire thing out loud and on your feet. For a less important presentation, practice the opening, closing, and main transitions this way.

* *Modify as necessary.* An initial rehearsal will point out where the structure is weak, if you are missing transitions, and if you have too much material. In following rehearsals, you can then focus on polishing your delivery skills and building your comfort level when using visuals.

Check your timing.   Practicing out loud gives you the chance to time your presentation. Running overtime can annoy your audience and undercut your credibility. Don't subject the audience to your own time warp.

* *Cut material if necessary.* After your timed rehearsal, you may find that you have far too much material for the allotted time. If so, you need to edit content and eliminate some visuals.

* *Don't plan to speak the entire time.* If your rehearsal reveals that you end almost exactly on time, you still need to cut content. Factor in some time for responding to questions, possibly starting late, and for your audience to understand your visuals.

* *Adjust timing as necessary.* Prepare yourself to adjust timing further, if necessary, during your presentation. If you run short on time, do not rush through your entire talk. Instead, plan to cut details and emphasize your main points.

2. Practice with your visual aids.

Also practice your ability to integrate your visual aids professionally and gracefully into the flow of your presentation.

Familiarize yourself with the equipment.   Become extremely comfortable with the equipment you have decided to use. Practice is especially important with high-tech visuals, visuals you haven't used much before, or visuals to be used in a new location or country.

- *Rehearse.* Don't lose credibility by fumbling with your visuals. Instead, practice repeatedly, especially with high-tech options. Touch the equipment: actually set it up, turn it on, press the buttons, use the remote, insert the video, flip the pages, position the slides, and so on. Remember that each model of equipment has different quirks, from placement of the power switch to availability of spare bulbs.

- *Prepare a backup plan* in case your equipment fails.

Introduce each visual.   Visuals do not speak for themselves; it's your job to help them communicate your message.

- *State your transition, then the main message.* Before you show a visual, first state your transition out loud, and then deliver the main message of the visual. For example, you might say as your transition: "So what were the sales results for the last quarter?" Then, stop talking and put up your visual. Once the audience can see it, you explain the main point as follows: ". . . Here you'll see that the Southwest office reached their $6 million dollar goal."

- *Give the audience time.* Be sure to give the audience enough time to comprehend and connect with each visual. Remember your audience has never seen your visuals before; therefore, it will take them longer to grasp the meaning of each visual than it will take you.

- *Explain complex visuals.* When showing complex visuals, introduce the main idea and then explain the meanings of colors, axis, or any symbols you've used. When possible, "build" complex charts and diagrams (as discussed on page 76) so you can provide this kind of explanation as you build the visual.

- *Cue the audience.* Don't assume the audience knows where they are supposed to look. Tell them. Show them. Or do both.

Don't let your visuals distract the audience.

- *Get rid of "old news."* Once you are done with an image, get it out of sight. Don't talk about a new idea while showing an old visual.

- *Avoid empty white screens.* Use the "blank screen" button or insert plain black slides into a slide show, or turn the overhead projector off if the blank screen would be showing for a long time.

- *Avoid becoming "magnetized" by your visuals.* Don't let your visuals become "eye-contact magnets." Talk to and look at your audience.

3. Prepare for your specific equipment.

In addition, here are a few ideas about how to meet the special challenges offered by the different kinds of equipment.

Computer-generated slide shows   (1) Use the cueing techniques computers offer. For example, use "build and dim" (as explained on pages 70 and 76) to add each new bullet point or each part of a complex graph. Or, use bold arrows, boxes, or contrasting colors to cue the audience to look at a particular place on the screen. (2) Before the presentation, check the colors on the large screen and modify if needed; what you saw on your computer screen won't be the same as what you see on the large screen.

Flipbooks   (1) Tell the audience the purpose of the flipbook and how you will be using it during the presentation. Do you want them to read it in advance, during, or after the presentation? (2) Direct the audience to the specific page you are discussing ("On page . . ."; "On the next four pages . . .") (3) Introduce each new page: explain your color coding ("As you see, the green line represents . . ."); the chart elements ("Across the top of the matrix, we have listed the criteria . . . Down the side, we have identified the candidates . . ."); and point out the main message ("Note that the trend is . . ." "Contrast the . . . with the . . .") (4) Don't read from the flipbook. Talk to the audience, not the paper. If possible, put the flipbook on a table so you can gesture, and be sure to look up so you can make eye contact. (5) Remember that flipbook presentations are supposed to be flexible and interactive. Be responsive to your audience: for example, omit pages that turn out to be unnecessary; change the sequence of pages; or jump ahead if appropriate.

Overheads   (1) Frame your overheads so they are easier to handle and block the extra light; (2) Be sure you have the special kind of marking pens—not regular pens. (3) Figure out where to stand. Avoid standing next to the projector where you may block someone's view of the screen. Also, check to see if the projector arm is blocking anybody's view.

With overheads, pointing can be an effective way to cue the audience. (1) Back up to the screen and point to the exact word or figure you're discussing—not just in the general direction of the screen. (2) If possible, use your hand and not a pointer—so you can avoid fiddling with the pointer, banging it against the defenseless screen, "conducting" with it, and so on. If you must use a pointer because of the placement of the screen, then put it down when you are not using it. (3) Point with the hand closest to the screen to avoid reaching across your body and turning your back to the audience. (4) When using lots of text visuals, try to stand to the left of the screen, so you can point to the beginning of the line, rather than the end of it.

Flipcharts   (1) Use thick markers and highly visible colors; have spare markers nearby. (2) Write the message titles ahead of time. (3) Flip pages over when you are done with them. (4) Leave a blank page between used ones. (5) Mark pages by turning up the bottom corner and noting the page topic in pencil so you can easily find and flip back to the page you need without looking through the entire pad of paper. (6) Bring masking tape if you want to post pages around the room or use them later. (7) Keep audience eye contact. Either stop talking, write, then look at the audience to discuss what you've written, or write when someone else is speaking—but try to look at the speaker as long as possible before breaking the connection and to look back afterwards to confirm that you got it right. (8) Point with the hand closest to the flipchart to avoid reaching across your body and turning your back to the audience.

III. MANAGE YOUR NERVOUS SYMPTOMS.

If speaking before a group makes you nervous, you are not alone. Surveys report that public speaking is the number one fear in the United States, more frightening than snakes, heights, loneliness—and even death. Nervous feelings are the result of adrenaline pumping through your body. Some common manifestations of speech anxiety include butterflies in the stomach, a pounding heart, sweaty palms, cold hands, a dry mouth, memory loss, shaking limbs, fidgeting fingers, a quivering voice, a rapid heartbeat, and blushing.

The good news is that many of these physical manifestations are not visible to the audience; therefore, presenters usually look better than they feel. The audience can't see a rapid heartbeat or sweaty palms. They may not even notice momentary memory loss. Instead of berating yourself for feeling nervous then, try to regard the adrenaline as a positive element, since your delivery might be flat without it. In addition, experiment with the options described in this section until you find the one, or the combination, that works best for you.

I. General techniques

Start by using the following methods to get started on increasing your confidence.

Identify your nervous symptoms.   First of all, figure out what symptoms affect you, grouping them as to whether they are visible or audible to the audience.

- *Body language:* If your visible symptoms are related to body language, review the material on body language at the beginning of this chapter (pages 84–91) and then try some of the physical relaxation techniques described later in this chapter (pages 100–101).

- *Vocal traits:* If your symptoms relate to vocal traits, review the material about rate, volume, and breathing patterns (pages 89–91) and then look at the vocal advice (page 101).

Prepare and rehearse. The most important way to enhance your delivery is through practice and rehearsal.

- *Follow the process outlined in this book.* If you have "aimed," structured, designed good visuals, and refined your delivery, you will find your confidence increasing and your nervousness decreasing. Knowing that you are well prepared should help calm you down.

- *Practice your delivery.* Once you know what you want to say, be sure to practice your presentation. Practice does not mean sitting and silently familiarizing yourself with your presentation content. Knowing something and saying it are two entirely different matters. Effective practice means rehearsing out loud, on your feet, using the same nonverbal behaviors as you would during the actual presentation. If the presentation is important, practice the entire thing, preferably in the room where you'll be presenting. If it is less important, practice the following three items out loud and on your feet: your opening, your closing, and your major transitions.

  Rehearsal is especially helpful for people who fear "memory loss moments." By saying your points out loud, you can then rely on "muscle memory." Without necessarily recalling the exact words, you will automatically say something similar to what you said during your rehearsal.

- *Practice with your visuals.* Rehearse at least once with your equipment, well before the actual presentation, so you can make changes in handouts and other visuals as needed. If possible, rehearse with the actual equipment you'll be using and in the room you'll be in.

- *Get some feedback.* If possible, videotape your rehearsal so you can hear and see yourself from the audience's perspective. You may also want to ask someone to watch your rehearsal. Ask this person not to focus on anything that can't be adjusted in the time remaining before your real presentation.

- *Don't try to memorize.* Although you might think that memorizing your presentation makes the task easier, don't do it. In some cases, memorizing the first 30 seconds may help you get though opening jitters, but writing out your talk word for word will make you sound artificial. Instead, see the suggestions on pages 93–94.

2. Physical techniques

The following set of techniques is based on the assumption, shared by many athletes and performers, that by relaxing yourself physically, you will calm yourself down mentally. Experiment with some of the following suggestions until you find one that is useful for you.

Exercise   One way to relax is to exercise before a presentation. Many people calm down following the physical exertion of calisthenics, jogging, tennis, or other athletic activities.

Breathing exercises   Controlled breathing exercises are another effective way to calm down. Remember that the out-breath is the calming breath. Avoid breathing too fast, emphasizing the in-breath, or hyperventilating.

- *Emphatic out-breathing:* First breathe in normally through your nose. Then, breathe out through your mouth—either with an audible sigh; a series of short, staccato bursts of air; or one long, continuous stream of air released as slowly as possible.

- *Metered breathing:* In this exercise, first, breathe in and out slowly and comfortably to the count of four in and four out, like a metronome. Then, keeping the same metronome pace, breathe in to the count of four, hold to the count of four, and breathe out to the count of eight.

Progressive relaxation exercise   Developed by psychologist Edmund Jacobson, progressive relaxation involves tensing and relaxing muscle groups. To practice this technique:

- *Set aside about 20 minutes of undisturbed time* in a comfortable, darkened place where you can lie down.

- *Tense and relax* each muscle group in turn. To tense a muscle group, clench vigorously for a full five to seven seconds. To relax a muscle group, release the tension very quickly and enjoy the warmth of relaxation. The muscle groups are hands, arms, forehead, neck and throat, upper back, lower back, chest, stomach, buttocks, thighs, calves, and feet.

- Repeat the procedure at least twice, tensing and relaxing each group of muscles in turn.

Relaxation for specific body parts   For some people, stage fright manifests itself in certain parts of the body—for example, tensed shoulders, quivering arms, or fidgety hands. Here are some exercises to relax specific body parts:

- *Relax your neck and throat.* Gently roll your neck from side to side, front to back, chin to chest, or all the way around.
- *Relax your shoulders.* Raise one or both shoulders as if you were shrugging. Then roll them back, then down, then forward. After several repetitions, rotate in the opposite direction.
- *Relax your arms.* Shake out your arms, first only at the shoulders, then only at the elbow, finally letting your hands flop at the wrist.
- *Relax your hands.* Repeatedly clench and relax your fists. Start with an open hand and close each finger one by one to make a fist; hold the position; then release.

Vocal relaxation   Some nervous symptoms affect your voice, such as cracking, quivering, or dry mouth. Here are some general suggestions for keeping your voice in shape:

- *Be awake.* Wake up several hours before your presentation to provide a natural warm-up period for your voice.
- *Take a hot shower.* A hot shower will wake up your voice, allowing the steam to soothe a tired or irritated set of vocal cords.
- *Avoid milk.* Avoid consuming milk or other dairy products before you speak. Dairy products tend to coat the vocal cords, which may cause problems during your presentation.
- *Drink warm liquids* to soothe a tired voice. Ideal candidates are herbal tea and warm water with lemon. Warm liquids with caffeine are fine for your voice, but they might increase your heart rate.
- *Get enough sleep* the night before your presentation. Your voice needs rest, too.
- *Hum* to warm up your voice. Start slowly and quietly, gradually adding a full range of pitches.
- *Breathe.* Before the presentation, try one of the breathing exercises described on the page at left. During the presentation, remember to breathe deeply.
- *Drink water.* During the presentation, have a glass of water nearby. If you have dry mouth, pause and take a drink of water as needed.

3. Mental techniques

Some speakers find that mental relaxation techniques work better for them—that mental relaxation causes physical relaxation. Here are various mental relaxation techniques to try until you find one that works for you.

"Think positive."   Base your thinking on the Dale Carnegie argument: To feel brave, act as if you are brave. To feel confident, act as if you are confident. Or repeat positive words or phrases, such as "poised, perfect, prepared, poised, perfect, prepared." Try to consider the adrenaline that may be causing nervous symptoms as a positive energy. All speakers may feel butterflies in their stomachs; effective speakers get those butterflies to fly in formation, thereby transforming negative into positive energy.

Think nonjudgmentally.   Describe your behavior ("I notice a monotone") rather than judging it ("I have a terrible speaking voice!") Then change the behavior by thinking rationally or using a positive self-picture, both of which are described below.

Think rationally.   Avoid being trapped in the "ABCs of emotional reactions," as developed by psychologist Albert Ellis.
   Here are the ABCs of emotional reactions:

A: **A**ctivating event (such as a nervous speaking gesture) sparks an irrational

B: **B**elief system (such as "What a disaster!" or "I must be absolutely perfect in every way; if I'm not perfect, then I'm terrible" or "It's a terrible catastrophe if something goes wrong"), which causes

C: **C**onsequences (such as anxiety or depression).

Transcend these ABCs by

D: **D**isputing irrational belief systems with rational thought (such as "Now that I'm aware of that gesture, I can gradually eliminate it" or "I don't demand perfection from other speakers" or "My equipment just broke, but that's not the end of the world. I'll go on naturally instead of getting flustered.").

Create a positive self-picture. Many speakers find that positive self-pictures work better than positive words.

- *Visualize yourself as a successful speaker,* including hearing positive comments or applause. Act out this visualization in your head. Then act out the role of the person you've been visualizing.

- *Use a positive video picture.* Work with a videotape of yourself giving a real or simulated presentation. Freeze the video at the point where you really like yourself, where you look and sound strong. Recreate that image when it's time for your next presentation.

- *Think of yourself as the guru.* Remind yourself that you know your subject matter.

Visualize a calm scene. Relax by conjuring up in your mind a visual image of a positive and pleasant object or scene.

- *Imagine a scene.* On each of the several days before the presentation, close your eyes and imagine a beautiful, calm scene, such as a beach you have visited. Imagine the details of temperature, color, and fragrance, concentrating on the image and excluding all else. Try repeating positive phrases, such as "I feel warm and relaxed" or "I feel content."

- *Juxtapose the stress.* A few days before the presentation, visualize the room, the people, and the stress. Then, distance yourself and relax by visualizing the pleasant image.

Connect with the audience. Try to see your audience as real people.

- *Meet them and greet them.* When people are arriving, greet them, get to know some of them. Then, when you're speaking, find those people in the audience and feel as if you're having a one-to-one conversation with them.

- *Remember that they are individuals.* Even if you can't greet the people in the audience, think of them as individual people, not as an amorphous audience. As you speak, imagine you are conversing with them.

- *"Befriend" the audience.* Picture yourself in your own home, enthusiastically talking with old friends. Try to maintain a sense of warmth and goodwill. This altered perception can not only diffuse your anxiety, but also increase your positive energy.

4. Last-minute techniques

When it's actually time to deliver the presentation, here are a few relaxation techniques that you can use at the last minute—and even as you speak.

Last-minute physical relaxation   Obviously, you cannot start doing push-ups or practice humming as you're about ready to begin speaking. Fortunately, however, there are some other techniques that you can use to relax your body at the last minute—techniques no one can see you using.

- *Isometric exercises:* Clench and then quickly relax your muscles. For example, you might press or wiggle your feet against the floor, one hand against your other hand, or your hands against the table or chair; you might clench your fists, thighs, or toes. Then, quickly relax the muscles you just clenched.

- *Deep-breathing exercises:* Inhale slowly and deeply from the diaphragm, then exhale slowly and completely. Pause between breaths. Try breathing in through your nose and out through your mouth. Or, try imagining you are breathing in "the good" and breathing out "the bad." Avoid hyperventilating or shallow breathing from your upper chest.

Last-minute mental relaxation   Also at the last minute, you may dispel stage fright mentally by using what behavioral psychologists call "internal dialogue," which means, of course, talking to yourself. Here are some examples:

- *Give yourself a pep talk.* "What I am about to say is important" or "I am ready" or "They are just people."

- *Play up your audience's reception.* "They are interested in my topic" or "They are a friendly group of people."

- *Repeat positive phrases.* "I'm glad I'm here; I'm glad you're here" or "I know I know" or "I care about you."

Relaxing as you speak   Finally, here are four techniques that you can use to relax even as you speak.

- *Speak to the interested listeners.* There are always a few kind souls out there who nod, smile, and generally react favorably. Especially at the beginning of your presentation, look at them, not at the people reading, staring out the window, or yawning. Seeing the positive listeners will increase your confidence and soon you will be looking throughout the room.

- *Talk to someone in the back row.* At the beginning of the presentation, take a deep breath and talk to the person in the back row to force your volume and breathing.

- *Remember that you probably look better than you think you do.* Your nervousness is probably not as apparent to your audience as it is to you. Experiments show that even trained speech instructors do not see all the nervous symptoms speakers think they are exhibiting. Managers and students watching videotapes of their performances regularly say, "Hey, I look better than I thought I would!"

- *Concentrate on the here and now.* Focus on your ideas and your audience. Forget about past regrets and future uncertainties. You have already analyzed what to do—now just do it wholeheartedly. Enjoy communicating your information to your audience, and let your enthusiasm show.

In closing, we hope we have provided you with two useful frameworks for designing effective presentations:

- *The AIM Strategy Framework,* covered in Part I, to (1) analyze your audience, (2) identify your intent, and (3) make your message memorable.

- *The SVN Implementation Framework,* covered in Part II, for (4) structure, (5) visuals, and (6) nonverbal delivery.

In addition, we hope that the Index will prove useful for any specific questions you may have and that the Bibliography will guide you to find any further information you may need.

BIBLIOGRAPHY

This bibliography serves both to acknowledge our sources and to provide readers with references for additional reading.

Aristotle. *The Art of Rhetoric.* New York: Penguin Books, 1991.

Bolton, R. *People Skills: How to Assert Yourself, Listen to Others, and Resolve Conflicts.* New York: Simon & Schuster, 1986.

Buzan, T. *The Mind Map Book.* New York: Penguin Books, 1996.

Cialdini, R. *Influence: The Psychology of Persuasion.* New York: Quill William Morrow, 1993.

Howell, J. *Tools for Facilitating Meetings.* Seattle: Integrity Publishing, 1995.

Knapp, M., and J. Hall. *Nonverbal Communication in Human Interaction,* 4th ed. Orlando: Harcourt Brace, 1996.

Kosslyn, S. *Elements of Graph Design.* New York: W. H. Freeman and Company, 1994.

Minto, B. *The Pyramid Principle: Logic in Writing, Thinking, and Problem Solving.* London: Minto International, Inc., 1995.

Munter, M. "Cross-Cultural Communication for Managers." *Business Horizons,* May/June 1993.

____ *Guide to Managerial Communication,* 5th ed. Upper Saddle River, NJ: Prentice Hall, 2000.

Rodenberg, P. *The Right to Speak: Working with the Voice.* New York: Routledge, 1992.

Rose, C. *Accelerated Learning for the 21st Century.* New York: Dell, 1998.

Tufte, E. *The Visual Display of Quantitative Information.* Cheshire, CT: Graphics Press, 1992.

White, J. *Color for Impact.* Berkeley, CA: Strathmore Press, 1996.

Williams, R. *The Non-Designers Design Book: Design & Typographic Principles for the Visual Novice.* Berkeley, CA: Peachpit Press, 1994.

Yates, J. "Persuasion: What the Research Tells Us." Cambridge, MA: Sloan School, Massachusetts Institute of Technology, 1992.

Zelazny, G. *Say It With Presentations: How to Design and Deliver Successful Business Presentations.* New York: McGraw-Hill, 2000.

Index